AF441644

I dedicate this book to my Grandchildren, in the hopes that MY tiny steps in Life may inspire THEM to take great strides in theirs.

With all my love.

Acknowledgements

This book would not have been possible without the support and contributions of the most important people in my life ...

To my husband, Julian, whose invaluable suggestions and insights guided me through the writing process.

And, to my three amazing children, who helped me recall precious memories and supported me every step of the way.

Your encouragement made this journey a joy.

Contents Page

Chapter 1

Memories of a Man

In the bustling city of Bombay, as it was known during my childhood, there lay a charming neighbourhood called Mahim. Back then, Mahim wasn't as crowded, and the streets weren't packed with vehicles. This place was special for several reasons, but one of its main attractions was the beautiful St. Michael's Church. People from all over Bombay came here for the Novenas to Our Lady of Perpetual Succour, held every Wednesday from early morning until late at night.

Mahim was also known for its educational institutions. The Canossa Convent School for girls, managed by Italian nuns, was a notable landmark. There were two schools for boys: St. Michael's High School and Victoria High School. The area was a melting pot of all communities, living together in harmony.

Adjacent to Canossa School stood a lovely three-story building called "Regi Annexe," constructed in 1936. My parents lived on the first floor, and I spent the first 22 years of my life in that wonderful two-bedroom apartment. The main road ran alongside our building, and our street was aptly named Station Road, as it led directly to the Mahim Railway Station. Opposite Regi Annexe was a single-story chawl known as Rosary Building, and to the side was a sprawling Parsi Colony.

A narrow lane between our building and the school was where all the kids from our building gathered to play during the summer holidays. Our building housed eight Catholic families, so there were plenty of boys and girls. We played cricket, hockey, gilli danda, chain cook, cops and robbers, and kick the can. Those were the days when children enjoyed the outdoors, basking in the sun!

Childhood Home

My name is Freda Vaz, née Mathias, and I was born in 1954, in Mumbai, which was then called Bombay. My parents, Leo and Bridget Mathias, were my pillars. Dad was the only son among his siblings, with three sisters: Aunty Nina, Effie, and Bevinda (Ben). The two older sisters lived in Bombay, while the youngest, A. Ben, a spinster, resided in Siolim, Goa.

Dad owned a large, palatial house in Goa. Being the youngest, he had a special place in the family. We used to visit Goa for the May holidays, traveling by ship, which was always a thrilling and fun-filled experience. We spread out mats on the deck and enjoyed the journey, which took nearly a whole day. Back then, there was no electricity in Goa, making the nights quite eerie. We were fascinated by the retro soda bottles with marbles in the top, a novelty for us kids from Bombay. The elders would press down the marble to open the bottle, and it never ceased to amaze us.

The highlight of our Goa holidays was the mango season. Dad's house had many rooms, one of which was always filled with mangoes. The property boasted numerous fruit trees. However, the flooring of the house was made of cow dung, a traditional practice that helped keep the house cool. Being Bombay-born, we had to get used to it. The toilet was located outside, referred to as the "Piggy toilet" in Goa.

In 1970, when I accompanied Dad to Goa to sell the house, none of the sisters were interested in keeping it. He sold it to some Afrikaners. That trip was particularly sad for me because Dad had his first heart attack just after we arrived in Goa. He suffered from rheumatism, and the local doctor refused to administer his injection, fearing it would affect his heart. Dad used to sit up with a mattress rolled behind him and his legs dangling down. I used chicken feathers to apply a local mixture to his legs to relieve the pain. Eventually, Mom arrived and convinced the doctor to give the injection, taking full responsibility for the consequences. We hired a car and drove back to Bombay. In the end, Mom said Dad sold the house for a song.

Dad worked for NAFI, and we were raised in a strict, military-style environment where punctuality was paramount. Everything in our household ran like clockwork, a habit that I carry with me to this day:

Breakfast at 7:30 am

Lunch at 12:30 pm

Tea at 4:00 pm

Dinner at 9:00 pm

Dad went to the market every morning at 8:30 am. The moment he left; I would turn on the radio at full blast to enjoy some fantastic music on Radio Ceylon before school. I had to make sure to turn it down when I saw him returning. If I forgot, he'd say, "Why is the music so loud? Is this an Iranian restaurant?" Ha! Ha!

After we all started working, Dad handled our bank work. He worked part-time for Maniar Plastics in Chembur after retiring, a half-hour train ride away. He returned home around 6:00 pm and then went to the park to meet his friends. He had dinner at 8:00 pm and was in bed by 9:00 pm, though he only slept until midnight and was awake through the night, a habit from his NAFI days.

Dad was a math genius. He could solve my math problems in his head and give me the answer. I'd then hand him my textbook and ask, "Dad, can you solve it according to the book?" Ha! Ha! We also played cards, and he would calculate and tell me where I made mistakes. That's how we all learned to play cards, and we had many lovely times together.

He had an amazing memory for people's names and family trees, which drove my mother crazy. He'd say, "Biddy, do you remember him/her? Daughter/son of so and so?" My mother wasn't interested; she loved staying home with her kids. We'd laugh in the bedroom, imagining Mom's rising blood pressure. That was Dad! He remembered everyone, with the memory of an elephant.

Despite being stern, Dad had a fantastic sense of humour. One incident I recall is when Mom used snuff for her nose. He'd say, "Biddy, you buy Re.1 worth of snuff, but 75 paise is on the ground," making Mom scream, "Please get lost and leave me alone!" Ha! Ha! Ha!

He loved to tease her. She always woke up at seven in the morning. One day, he set the clock 15 minutes early. When she woke up, she realized she was up early and was furious. Ha! Ha!

April Fool's Day was another favourite of his. Our home had two entrances: one to the hall and another to the kitchen, which we called the back door. We didn't have a phone, but our neighbours did. If there was a call for us, they'd bang on our door with the latch and leave their door open for us to enter and take the call.

One day, Dad decided to fool me. He went from the front door to the back door, banged the latch, and then ran to the front door, yelling, "Freda, there's a call for you." I ran to the neighbour's door, but it was closed. Dad had a good laugh.

I decided to get back at him. Since he read the newspaper early in the morning and woke me up at 5:00 am to study for exams, I took the previous day's newspaper and placed it near the door. When he went to read it, I watched his puzzled expression as he wondered why the news was old. I laughed and said, "Dad, April Fool!" He burst out laughing. I was thrilled to have pranked him at least once.

Once, he returned from a funeral, and I asked, "Dad, how did he die?" He replied, "He had a heart." We all burst out laughing. Don't we all have a heart?

Daddy always made egg flip with brandy for me every time I was sick with a cough and cold. I used to enjoy the pampering. And today, I think of him and miss it.

Tragically, Dad had a massive heart attack and died two days before his 70th birthday on September 4, 1980. I was in Saudi Arabia at the time and couldn't attend the funeral. I cried a lot because I was his pet daughter. "He had a heart too, but he was a wonderful person."

Daddy and Mom
on my Wedding Day

Dancing with Daddy
at my Engagement party

Parra House in Goa

Daddy's Girl

Chapter 2

My Mother, Bridget

My mom, Bridget, was a stunning woman who everyone said resembled Queen Elizabeth. She was deeply God-fearing and whenever anyone needed prayers, they would call her. She would light a lamp and pray fervently.

Mom was incredibly talented. She loved stitching, painting, and cooking. I loved sitting by her side, watching her stitch. She took orders for clothes, and I was always there, watching her work her magic with the needle. Before starting any stitching, she always said a prayer. She stitched all our clothes and often took us to the market to buy fabric. She would buy one type of fabric and make matching outfits for all of us. She started in the afternoon and by evening, the dress would be neatly hung on a hanger. Her stitching was impeccable. She always said, "The wrong side should look as good as the right side." Ha! Ha!

Mom also did cross-stitch work, but what fascinated me most was her talent for fairy work, as it was called back then. I still have a set of her cushion covers that I use to this day. It's sad how these crafts have faded away. She also painted chicken feathers and made hats for sale. They looked so pretty!

One of her hobbies was planting different coloured roses. She would travel all the way into town to buy new grafts and plant them in her pots, spending hours admiring the beauty of her flowers. Another passion of hers was collecting stamps from different countries. She amassed a collection of nearly 5,000 stamps, which I still treasure.

Mom was originally from Parra, a village in Goa, about a ten-minute drive from Mapusa. My grandparents had a grand house there, with mosaic tile floors and Venetian glass windows. My grandfather worked for the railways and provided well for the family. We loved visiting the Parra house and have many cherished memories of our time there.

Mom came from a large family; she was one of ten children, with five brothers and five sisters. One sister died very young. Mom was third in line. There was Uncle John, Aunty Ruby, Bridget (Mom), Uncle Phillip, Aunty Bonny, Uncle Ferdie,

Uncle Charlie, Uncle Celo, and Aunty Winnie. My youngest daughter always jokes, "They had no TV in those days, so they made babies." Ha! Ha!

Growing up with five brothers, Mom was a tomboy. She loved climbing trees and playing all the boys' sports. She even had a passion for horse racing. Despite her tomboyish nature, she was the first to get married among her siblings, which meant I had many cousins who were younger than me.

I don't have any brothers, only three sisters: Joyce, Jeanette, and Audrey. There's a six-year gap between Jeanette and me, and another seven-year gap between me and Audrey. We affectionately called each other Joey, Johnny, Freddy, and Bulu.

Mom loved listening to our stories when we returned from school or work. She knew all our friends by name, even though she had never met them. She insisted on this daily ritual of sharing our day's events with her. It's a tradition I've continued with my children. Every time they come home, they share their stories with me, and it always brightens my day.

Mom was also very strict. Lying was not tolerated, and if you were caught, you'd get a whack. Our house had two bedrooms that you could walk around in a loop. When Mom came to discipline us, we'd run around in circles. She'd say, "For every round, you'll get one more whack," so we'd stop and take the punishment. It's funny in retrospect, but it was serious business back then. Ha! Ha!

She demanded absolute silence during her afternoon naps. If we disturbed her, she'd fling her slipper at us. Ha! Ha! I guess that's where I get it from. I don't like being disturbed during my afternoon naps either!

I have fond memories of Mom's cooking. Some of my favourites were Green Ball curry, which won me first prize twice—once at the Taj Goa and another time at a cooking contest in Mapusa. She also made delicious Tongue roast, Sorpotel, potato chops (which were huge), Irish stew, and Goan sweets like Tizaan, guava cheese, peanut toffee, and banana fritters.

The best times were during Christmas when we made sweets. We'd all sit around the table making neureos and kulkuls, singing at the top of our voices. It was so much fun. We each took turns stirring the batter for the Christmas cake. Mom also made amazing grape wine, which we all loved!

Christmas week was truly magical. I'd wait for Mom and Dad to take their afternoon naps so I could sneak into the kitchen and raid the big basket full of sweets. I felt like a little thief, but doesn't food always taste better when eaten on the sly?

Mom's cooking was legendary. On my wedding day, she made the famous Goan sweet "Dodol" after hours of stirring. She left it to cool, and since we all had to go to church for my Wedding Mass, my youngest sister's friend stayed behind to watch the house. Mom instructed her to give anyone who came by a piece of Dodol. But the friend found it so delicious that she kept taking more and more. When we came back, we discovered she had almost finished it all! Mom and my sisters were furious, but we laugh about it now.

Mom passed away on November 3, 2004, on her birthday. She had a heart attack, but she was prepared for it. I believe I have an angel up there, looking after me.

Bridget, my mother, was a beautiful, talented, and loving woman who left an indelible mark on all our lives. Her legacy lives on in the skills she passed down, the traditions she instilled, and the love she gave us. She may no longer be with us physically, but her spirit continues to guide and inspire me every day.

Mother and Me

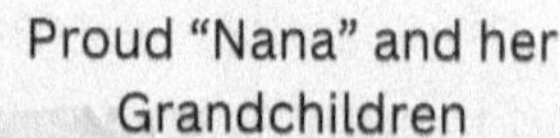

Proud "Nana" and her Grandchildren

Mother and her 4 girls
From left: Joyce, Audrey, Mum, Me & Jenni

Top left: Uncle Charlie, Aunty Winnie, Aunty Rubie, Boodie girl, Aunty Yvette, Uncle Phillip, Mummy, Aunty Bonnie, Uncle Omar
Middle left: Uncle Bernard, Aunty Rita, Nana, Uncle Ferdie, Aunty Muriel, Grandpapa, Uncle Charles
Front Line: Daddy and the kids

Mother Of Mine

Chapter 3

Joyce, or Joey as we called her, was my eldest sister and a truly lovable person. She had a warm, infectious personality that made everyone around her feel cherished.

One amusing incident from our childhood stands out vividly in my memory. Joyce was in school, and I was very young at the time. One day, she left for school with her uniform on top of her nightie. We ran to the balcony, trying to call her back. Mom started shouting, "Girlie, can you please call that girl?" since all the school children were on their way to school. Eventually, Joyce came back home, completely oblivious to what she had done. We all had such a hearty laugh about it once she realized.

Joyce didn't complete her SSC due to health reasons, but that didn't stop her from pursuing her passions. She loved dressing up in Indian wear and looked stunning in traditional outfits. She worked in the film industry, with Chetan

Anand as her boss, and even appeared as an extra in the movie "Hakikat." She took me to see some movie shoots, and that's how I got to know the names of Indian actors and actresses, watched Hindi movies, and learned Hindi songs. Joyce also loved dancing and was fantastic at the Jive. And of course, she loved playing cards, a skill we all picked up from Dad.

I remember going for early morning runs at 5:00 AM with Joyce and Jenny. It was during one of these runs that Joyce met Joe. They dated for the next 13 years before getting married in Kuwait. Joyce moved to Kuwait, and they had two sons, Jeldon and Jayde. When I visited Kuwait, they asked me to be Jeldon's godmother, which was a great honour.

In 1999, I was comfortably watching TV at home in Goa when I saw a beautiful advertisement for a lottery in Dubai, with the grand prize being a one-kilo gold bar. The images of Dubai's grandeur captivated me, and I wished I could visit. Miraculously, not long after, Joyce's son Jeldon sent me a message: "Aunt Freda, I'm sending you a ticket to come to my wedding in Dubai." I was over the moon!

Mom, Jenny, Audrey, and I went to Dubai for the wedding. My sister Jenny sang a solo for the Mass, and I surprised Jeldon and Wendy by singing Shania Twain's "You're Still the One" for their first dance. Jeldon was thrilled. During our stay, we were invited to the palatial house of one of Jeldon's Arab friends. He presented Wendy with a huge diamond ring. The host was surprised to see how much I enjoyed the Arabic food, and I had to explain that I spent 13 years in Saudi Arabia and loved the cuisine.

We did a lot of shopping in Dubai, which was not as modern as it is today but still had hypermarkets. With two shopaholic sisters, every day was an adventure.

One day, we received a call from Jeldon, who was in London. He asked us to check on his parents, who were in Goa at the time, because he felt something was wrong. When we reached their house, we found that Joe had passed away from a heart attack. Joyce was devastated and soon began to exhibit strange behaviour. She didn't know what she was saying or doing, and eventually, she had to be placed in an aged care home. She couldn't recognize anyone, which was heartbreaking to see. It was painful to watch someone who had always been so full of life and laughter reach such a state.

I didn't have many years with Joyce, as she was eight years older than me. She passed away in 2022, a very sad time for all of us. Whenever she visited Goa from Bombay, she stayed for two months. Every afternoon at exactly 3:00 PM, there would be a knock on the door. She'd bring snacks, and we'd play cards till 4:00 PM, have tea and snacks, and then continue playing till 6:00 PM. Whenever she had a lot of diamonds in her hand, she'd sing "Diamonds are forever, forever, forever." We all laughed so much. She lived just a lane away from my house.

I miss those times we spent together. Her favourite saying was, "You can say that again!" Joyce's presence brought so much joy and laughter into our lives. Her memory continues to be a source of comfort and nostalgia for me, reminding me of the warmth and fun she always radiated.

Jeldon, Joyce, Jayde and Joe

Jeldon's Wedding

Joe & Joyce

Chapter 4

Johnny

Jenny, or Johnny as we affectionately called her, was my second sister and six years older than me. She had a lively spirit and a passion for reading that was almost legendary in our household. Jenny would sneak her novels into her study books, finding any chance to dive into a story. Her book collection was vast and completely out of my reach, a treasure trove of adventures and romances that I could only dream of exploring.

When Jenny started working, she initially became a secretary for Avery, and later on, she secured a position as the secretary to the company secretary of NOCIL (National Organic Chemical Industries Ltd). Her job came with perks, and every time she received a bonus, she would bring home an array of delightful goodies. We eagerly anticipated these moments, as she would treat us to baskets of strawberries, imported cheeses, and other delicious treats.

Her bonuses were like mini celebrations for the whole family.

Jenny loved to travel and explored the world on various holidays. Her travels inspired her fashion sense, and she always dressed impeccably, with a wardrobe full of stylish outfits and matching accessories. One day, I couldn't resist the temptation and "borrowed" her red velvet bag to take to work. Jenny left for work before me, catching the bus, while I took the train. However, as I walked to my office, I heard someone calling my name. It was Jenny, pointing at the bag from her bus window. I knew I was in for it when I got home! Ha! Ha!

Music was another one of Jenny's passions. All four of us sisters loved to sing, and we often sang together in the church choir. Jenny continued her singing throughout her life, joining various choirs and enjoying a fulfilling singing career. However, her musical journey wasn't without its humorous and embarrassing moments.

One particularly memorable incident occurred during a choir feast. Jenny was asked to sing a solo, and the choir sang from the loft. She was told to go down and sing, so she headed for the altar, where the only microphone was. As she stood there, waiting for the organist to start, she noticed everyone gesticulating wildly. Completely puzzled, she began to pray, hoping for some divine intervention. Suddenly, she spotted our aunt in the first pew, pointing to a microphone below. Sheepishly, she stepped down to the correct microphone and sang. The embarrassment was palpable, and she never heard the end of it from the other choristers!

Another funny moment happened when Jenny's nephew, who was five years old at the time, attended the Christmas midnight Mass at St. Michael's Church in Mahim. Despite living in the next town, Bandra, Audrey and her husband loved coming to this Mass. During communion, Jenny sang a solo of "O Holy Night." After she finished, her nephew stood up, clapped his hands vigorously, and shouted, "Aunty Tanni!" She was mortified, wanting to disappear as everyone in the choir loft giggled and the entire congregation, including the priest, looked up to see what was happening. Despite the embarrassment, it was the best compliment she ever received.

Jenny also had some remarkable experiences with our Mom's deep faith. Mom always mentioned that she talked to God the Father, and while we believed her, it was when she said He talked back that truly caught our attention. One such incident occurred when Jenny went to the doctor for her persistent cough and cold. The doctor suggested a blood test, and both she and Mom were anxious about the results. Thankfully, the test revealed nothing serious; she was simply lacking calcium and needed a series of injections.

Excited to share the good news, Jenny rushed home. But as soon as Mom opened the door, she announced she had good news herself. Mom said she had prayed, and God the Father told her, "There is nothing wrong with Jenny; she is only lacking in calcium." Jenny was flabbergasted. She still wonders if she would have had doubts had she delivered her news first. Mom's deep faith and frequent prayers were a constant source of amazement.

These are just a few stories that paint a picture of my sister Jenny. Her love for reading, her impeccable fashion sense, her passion for singing, and her unwavering faith are just a few facets of the vibrant personality that made her so special. Whether it was through her hilarious escapades or her profound moments of faith, Jenny brought a unique and unforgettable energy into our lives.

Jenni & Me

Jenni and her
Godchild,
Diahann Carroll

Jenni and the sisters

Jenni loves singing
in the church choir

Chapter 5

Bulu

Audrey, or Bulu as we fondly called her, is my youngest sister, seven years my junior. She was undoubtedly the smartest among us four sisters, and she was the only one in our family to complete her graduation.

I remember one particular incident vividly from when she was very young, and I was about 13 years old. I had taken her to the Canossa school compound to play, which was adjacent to our building. At precisely 7:00 PM, the school would release guard dogs to patrol the premises. As soon as I saw the dogs coming, I panicked and jumped over the wall, leaving Audrey behind. Unfortunately, she got bitten. My mother had to take her to Bandra, the next town over, which was a good hour's walk due to the curfew imposed during the Indo-Pakistan war. Audrey had to endure 14 injections in her stomach, one each day. To make the ordeal bearable, Mom bribed her with ice cream. That incident left me with a lingering fear of dogs, and I was deeply upset for a long time.

Despite this traumatic experience, Audrey grew up to be incredibly bright and always topped her class. Every time she excelled in school, she would ask for a parrot as a reward. We had so many parrots over the years, though they all either died or flew away. Ha! Ha!

Audrey eventually married her college friend, Robin Cooper, and moved to New Zealand. They have two boys, Gary and Gavin. Audrey runs her own Bible ministry there, conducting Bible classes and helping many people. She is also very talented and artistic, creating beautiful Christmas decorations, coasters, and resin works.

For my 50th birthday, Audrey sent me a ticket to New Zealand for a one-month holiday. The country was breathtaking. In that one month, I saw almost all of New Zealand. We visited the Auckland Harbor Bridge, the City of Sails, and One Tree Hill at Cornwall Park, which offered stunning views from the summit. The Blue Lake Reserve was mesmerizing, and we also explored a Māori Village, where I got to witness traditional dances and experience Māori culture firsthand. The hot mud pools and thermal mineral pools were a lot of fun too.

The Auckland Museum was a highlight, offering a glimpse into the region's history and culture.

Audrey and I also visited Lookout Point at Piha, with the Lion's Rock in the background. Huka Falls on the way to Taupo was another breathtaking sight. At SkyCity, the highest point in Auckland at 328 meters, I stood on the 38mm thick glass floor of the Sky tower, looking down at the city below. I even watched people bungee jump from the top of the tower. Hunua Falls at the Regional Park and the challenging bush walk we attempted were unforgettable experiences.

One of the most beautiful experiences was at Shakespeare Park, where I fed peacocks. It felt like a scene from a fairy tale. We also did some downtown shopping, where I found quality New Zealand gifts, souvenirs, jewellery, handicrafts, clothing, and accessories. Audrey took me kayaking in Coromandel, and we visited the stunning Hamilton Botanical Gardens.

We also visited the Waikato Region, where Robin was the Deputy General Manager. In Taupo, we explored the Hidden Valley and its breathtaking thermal springs. The walk up the ramp to the Arataki Information Centre was challenging, but I got a beautiful picture posing in front of the totem pole. Riding the Stagecoach Bus in Auckland was a nostalgic experience, and I cherished my souvenir of the trip by train.

Western Springs was incredibly scenic, and I loved feeding the ducks and swans. Mount Eden Crater offered another unique experience. The Mercury Bay Museum had so much to see, adding to the list of unforgettable memories. It was truly a memorable holiday.

In 2017, I returned to New Zealand with my sister Jenny for Audrey's son's wedding. All three of us practiced the hymns for the Mass together. Audrey was busy with the hall decorations and even made the wedding cake. After the Mass, we took a boat trip to the wedding reception, held in a luxurious venue. The reception included a ten-minute display of fireworks in the middle of the ocean, which was absolutely spectacular.

Following the wedding, Audrey and Robin took us on a road trip, visiting different places and staying in various hotels every day for almost a week. The scenery was out of this world. We went on a guided tour of underground stalagmite caves, where we sang to hear the echoes. It was an incredible experience.

By the end of the holiday, we were thoroughly exhausted. The next day, we flew back to India, receiving VIP treatment all the way since Robin worked for Air New Zealand at the airport. It was a long flight, and I slept through most of it. When I finally landed in Goa, it took me a few days to get over the jet lag.

Audrey's journey from being the youngest and smartest in our family to becoming a loving mother, talented artist, and dedicated Bible teacher in New Zealand is truly inspiring. Her intelligence, creativity, and strong faith have shaped her into the incredible person she is today. Our shared memories, from the joys of childhood to the adventures in New Zealand, are a testament to the strong bond we share and the remarkable journey we've experienced together.

Audrey & Robin

Chapter 6

My Life Story begins

Let's dive into the real story of my life. Growing up, I was quite the tomboy. I loved wearing shorts and mini dresses, whistling, and had an undeniable passion for cycling. I would save every bit of pocket money to rent a cycle for half an hour or an hour, depending on how much I had managed to save. Cycling without holding onto the handlebars was my thing, and my mother received numerous complaints from neighbours about my daring riding style. I always preferred a gent's bike over a ladies' one because it felt more adventurous. I learned to mount and ride like a true tomboy.

When I was eight, my mother asked me, "Would you like to learn ballet or singing?" I chose singing without a second thought. That's when my musical journey began. Back in 1962, we didn't have a radio, and I had never heard my mother sing. However, she taught me everything about singing from scratch, using only paper. I had to select a song, write it down, and then she would make me sing it, grading me on diction and stage performance. I had a powerful voice, and our parish church held a singing competition when I was eight. I entered and sang "Blue Moon."

Our practice sessions were intense. We closed all the doors and windows, and my mother used different coloured pencils to mark my mistakes. The first round focused on diction. She always said, "Every song has a story, so make sure the audience understands the words." I practiced for hours until she was satisfied. Next were facial expressions. I had to sing with feeling, which meant more coloured pencil marks and more practice. Once she was content, she set up a chair with an empty can as a makeshift microphone. I had to ensure I sang into the mic while engaging with the audience, especially the judges. Finally, I had to perfect my entrance, bow, and smile before standing in front of the mic and singing, remembering all the lessons on diction and expressions.

Without any musical background, I asked someone to accompany me, so I also practiced with them. I developed a good ear for music, and my mother's keen sense of detail helped me immensely. She even stitched a blue dress for the competition and made sure it was just right by having me stand on the windowsill to make sure that the judges couldn't see under my dress from where they sat!

Of course, she accompanied me to the competition, where I also sang "Santa Lucia" in the classical section. I won first place in both categories, which was exhilarating. One of the judges even gave me an anonymous cash prize. After that, I entered every singing competition in Bombay and consistently won first place, thanks to countless hours of practice.

I also participated in the Cadbury's competition at Byculla Mechanics and won first prizes in both jazz and classical categories. They invited me to sing at the Cadbury show on All India Radio. We didn't have a radio at home, so the day before my performance, my mother used her pocket money to buy our first Murphy Radio. Hearing myself on the radio at home was beyond thrilling.

At ten, I entered the Time and Talents Singing Competition, which had around 200 participants with no age limit. I made it to the finals, organized by the famous **Adi Marzban**. The three finalists had to perform at the Birla Auditorium for "The Sound of Music" show, and I won first place, receiving the "Julie Andrew's" trophy, an Eagle Flask, and a cash prize of Rs.100/-. They even asked me to perform for various shows at different auditoriums, singing with bands like **Goody Seervai or Maurice Concessio**. My performances of "Tonight's My Night" and "Looking for Love" by Connie Francis earned me the nickname "Connie Francis of Bombay."

Performing at ten and having my makeup done in the green room was a thrill. I got paid Rs. 40/- per show for a whole year. It was a significant opportunity to sing on big platforms alongside notable celebrities like Jimmy Pocha and his wife, Uma Pocha (sister of Usha Iyer).

Jimmy Pocha was a renowned Comedian on the Parsi stage and his wife, Uma Pocha was a singer best known for singing of the famous "Bombay Meri Hai!".

Despite the fame in my teens, I faced many ups and downs. Many boys wanted to get "friendly" with me. In those days, "friendly" meant spending time together, but nothing serious. My parents were very strict, so meeting boys was almost impossible. I did have a crush on a particular guy, and it was a fantastic feeling, though. We called it "Puppy Love." It was fun while it lasted, with the excitement of seeing him and the usual teenage giggles. However, jealousy among girls was a significant problem, and some friends betrayed me by reporting to my parents, resulting in me being grounded for a while.

In school, I participated in inter-school competitions and won prizes for my school, Canossa High School. I sang for the school assembly and could see my classrooms from my balcony at home.

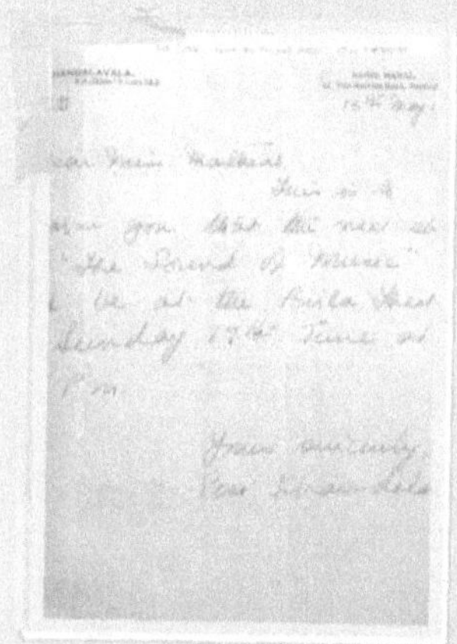

My 21st Birthday
(center in striped dress)

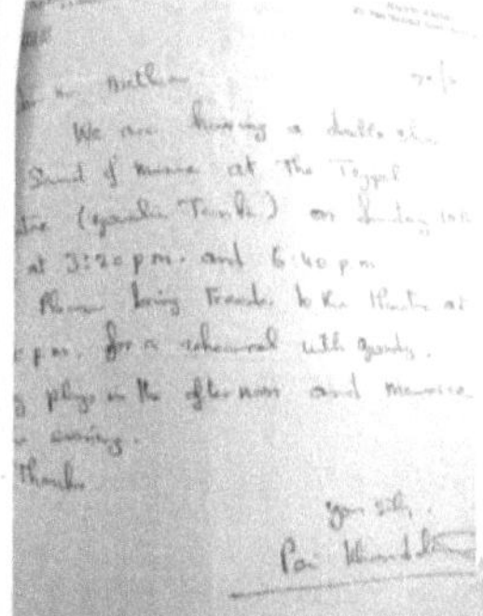

Letters inviting
me to shows to sing

The Les Amigos & me
at a wedding event!
(beside groom)

Sound of Music

Academically, I wasn't very strong, especially in Maths and Hindi. My dad always insisted, "You will complete your SSC (Secondary School Certificate)." Fortunately, I never failed a year. With a lot of prayers, I finally passed. Miracles do happen! Ha! Ha!

In 1970, we had the option to take typing instead of Mathematics for the SSC, which was a blessing. Just before finishing my SSC, the Jetliners band invited me to join them, but my dad said no. Several bands approached me, and I promised my dad I would join one when I turned 21. He was hesitant because I was only 17. Eventually, a famous drummer friend convinced my dad, assuring him he would take full responsibility for picking me up and dropping me home after performances. That's when I began my career as a crooner.

I joined the "Les Amigos" dance band, singing at weddings and dances on Saturdays and Sundays while working weekdays. It was a dream come true, performing on stage in front of people who enjoyed my singing. I was the only crooner in Bombay who used the entire stage for showmanship. Back then, there was no TV, so what Beyoncé and Tina Turner did on stage wasn't even conceived of. I even whistled on stage, confusing the audience as they tried to figure out where the sound was coming from among the trumpet, saxophone, bass guitar, organ, and drums. It was hilarious! I looked forward to my Saturday and Sunday gigs.

My sister Joyce, who was in Kuwait, sent me beautiful materials to stitch amazing gowns. I loved dressing up and performed in gorgeous gowns, shararas, and even hot pants with boots. Every time a taxi came to pick me up, neighbours would gather on their balconies to see what I was wearing.

Besides weddings, we performed at Christmas, Easter, and Diwali shows. Often, we performed the first half of a show in one part of town and rushed to another location for the second half. It was exhausting but incredibly enjoyable, and I met many interesting people.

By this time, I was well-known in Bombay. When commuting to work by train from Mahim to Churchgate, a half-hour journey, groups of ladies—Catholics and Hindus—would compete to give me a seat and make me sing during the ride. I sang both English and Hindi songs, having watched many Hindi movies. My favourite actor was Rajesh Khanna, and I knew all the songs from his movies.

I also sang in the church choir, performing solos occasionally. All my sisters sang for church services too. Joyce sang alto while Jenny and I sang soprano. I was once invited by the famous Alfred Rose to sing Konkani songs, but I didn't know Konkani, so I had to decline.

Who would have thought I'd end up getting married and settling in Goa? Even though my Konkani is still not perfect, I manage to understand some of it. Ha! Ha!

Over the years, some parents have told me their kids were big fans of mine. One mother mentioned how her daughter would drag her to the balcony to see me whenever I passed by. Others say they still think of me whenever they hear "Tonight's My Night." Ha! Ha! Unfortunately, I've forgotten most of the words by now.

My singing career had its share of unfortunate incidents. At one wedding, a guest had a heart attack while dancing. At another, the wedding cake fell while the couple was cutting it, considered a bad omen. At yet another, the bride was visibly pregnant.

After weekend performances, I often ended up at the doctor's clinic due to late nights, dew, and cold drinks affecting my throat, resulting in frequent sore throats.

This chapter of my life, from being a tomboy to a singer, was filled with excitement, challenges, and unforgettable memories. Despite the ups and downs, the journey shaped me into who I am today, and I wouldn't trade those experiences for anything.

Chapter 7

A Bond Beyond Time

Among the many memories that have shaped my life, my friendship with Jeroo stands out as a bright and cherished chapter. We met at Claire's Institute, where we were learning shorthand and typing. From the very beginning, we connected on a deeper level, becoming inseparable. Our bond grew even stronger when we discovered that we both lived in Mahim, just a few minutes' walk from each other's homes.

After finishing our course, our professional paths took different directions, but our friendship remained steadfast. Jeroo landed a job at Tata Consultancy Services, while I started working for a Chartered Accountant, typing countless statements every day. Soon after, I moved on to a position at BASF. Despite our busy schedules, we managed to maintain our routine of taking the same train home.

Every day after work, my routine was almost ritualistic. I would come home, throw my bag down, and eagerly ask Mom what there was to eat. We would sit together for at least ten minutes, during which I would share all the stories from my day. This moment of connection with my mother was precious to me, a grounding point before I rushed out again.

As soon as I had finished my quick meal, I would head out to meet Jeroo for our evening walks. These walks were more than just a way to stay fit; they were our time to catch up, share dreams, and support each other through the ups and downs of life. Whether it was a joyful event or a frustrating day at work, we knew we could rely on each other for understanding and comfort.

Our evening walks often took us to Mahim Beach, where we would buy either Bhelpuri, Falooda or Ragada etc. We would sit on the rocks and chat while the stress of the day slowly melted away. We talked about our ambitions, our worries, and everything in between. By the time we returned home, we felt lighter, our spirits lifted by the simple act of sharing our burdens.

Jeroo's Mum made the most delicious Dhansak dish. Every time I came down to India for my vacation, Jeroo would give me a huge parcel of Dhansak masala, the delicious Parsi dried fruit pickle and some Parsi sweets. The kids would be thrilled every time I made Dhansak in Saudi Arabia. It was finger licking yummy!

Even after Jeroo got married to Vispi one year after me, we stilled exchanged a lot of goodies.

Over the years, our lives continued to intertwine in beautiful ways. We celebrated each other's successes and provided solace during hardships. Our friendship grew deeper and more resilient with each passing year. Even as our professional lives became more demanding, we made it a point to carve out time for each other.

As we navigated the different phases of our lives, our friendship adapted and grew stronger. When I became a mother, Jeroo was there to offer advice and support. She doted on my children as if they were her own, and they loved her dearly. Her presence added a richness to our family life that I will always treasure.

Our bond is a testament to the power of true friendship, and I cherish every moment we have shared.

In the present day, our lives have taken us on different paths geographically, but our connection remains as strong as ever. We stay in touch through phone calls, messages, and occasional visits. Each conversation feels like picking up right where we left off, regardless of how much time has passed.

As we continue to walk our individual paths, I know that our friendship will remain a cherished and enduring part of my story.

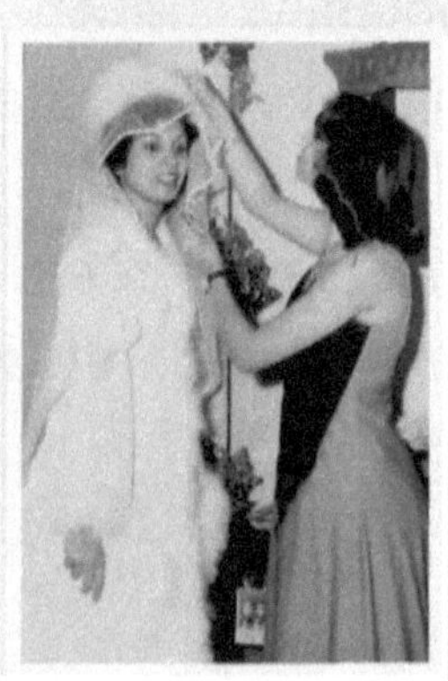

My Bridesmaid, Jeroo

Best Friends

Chapter 8

Unveiling Julian

Whenever I went to visit Jeroo, there was this guy who always hovered nearby, ready with some remark. "Your slip is showing" or "your buttons are open" were his favourites. It got to the point where, upon seeing him from a distance, I'd start checking myself to make sure everything was in order. Ha! Ha! Of course, I had no idea who he was or what his name might be.

One time, I was performing at the Church Fete at his parish, Victoria Parish, where they had a request program. People would select a song and pay for the band to sing it. I noticed that most requests were coming from the Nine Pin stall. After I finished my set, I came down from the stage, met my sister Joyce's fiancé Joe, and told him that someone at the Nine Pin stall was irritating me. Joe walked over, talked to the guy, and then introduced him to me as his friend Julian.

This was my first real conversation with Julian. Every time we met after that, we'd chat more. I didn't realize that he often walked up and down my street or sat in the restaurant opposite my house with his friends, all while I remained clueless about his interest in me.

One day, his friends challenged him to knock on my door and talk to me. He did, and my father answered the door. Julian made up a story about a church magazine, which allowed him to come inside for the first time. Later, I ran into him at the passport office. When he asked what I was doing there, I told him I was trying to get my passport. To my surprise, he offered to help, as he worked for Blue Skies Travel Agency. A couple of days later, he showed up at my house with my passport. We met again in town, and I clearly remember sharing a Russian salad at a restaurant.

Julian was six ft. tall and had attended Don Bosco's Boarding School in Matunga. He played the clarinet for the school band and sometimes the drums. He was the life of any party with his endless jokes, ensuring there was never a dull moment.

A few weeks later, it was my 21st birthday party, and I invited Julian. At the time, I was interested in someone else, but the moment Julian walked in, all my friends wanted to know if he was the one. I said, "No, he is just a friend."

But Julian kept calling me at the office during lunch hours. One day, feeling particularly down, I got a message from the receptionist that Julian had called to say he was leaving for Saudi Arabia. When he asked me out again, I finally said "Yes"! Of course, I had to ask my parents for permission since I'd never gone out for a late-night movie with a guy. They agreed, and that night marked the beginning of a new chapter in my life.

I said goodbye to Julian as he left for Riyadh in July 1975. His sister Justine and her husband were instrumental in taking him there. We started writing letters to each other, and I soon, I soon got tired of writing and decided to ask my sister Joyce, who was pregnant, if she could take me to Kuwait so I could be closer to Julian. She agreed but made me promise not to continue my singing career in Kuwait due to the responsibilities in an Arab country. Of course, she had to get Dad's permission, promising to look after me and ensure I worked.

We didn't tell Dad the real reason I wanted to go. Ha! Ha! Dad agreed, provided I used my own money for the flight and visa, which I had thanks to his lessons on saving. I had to create an entirely new wardrobe due to the conservative fashion in Kuwait. I remember Dad saying, "Freda, I hope you know you've emptied your bank account?" on the day I left.

On March 3, 1976, I left for Kuwait. At the airport, I looked around, and my sister asked, "What are you looking for?" I replied, "I was hoping to see Julian at the airport." She laughed and explained that Julian needed a visa to come from Saudi Arabia to Kuwait. How was I to know? My geography was terrible!

A lot of people in Kuwait heard I was there and wanted me to sing, but I had to decline due to the promise I made to my sister. I started working in her office to replace her while she prepared for maternity leave. Still, there was no sign of Julian and no letters either. I was so upset that I spent all my money to come to Kuwait for nothing. I decided to write him a stern letter expressing my frustration.

The very afternoon I posted the letter, Julian called. I was thrilled! He explained that he had been transferred to Jeddah for a short period and hadn't received my letters. He had just returned to Riyadh and discovered I was in Kuwait, prompting him to call me immediately. I felt terrible about the letter I had sent and asked him to tear it up without reading it. He laughed, and we moved on.

Eid holidays soon arrived in Kuwait. One evening after dinner, my sister and I were watching TV, and my brother-in-law Joe went to throw out the trash. Suddenly, I heard him say, "Hi Julian!" I turned pale and ran into the kitchen, trembling.

Julian came in, hugged and kissed me, and all I could do was cry tears of joy and shock. He had surprised me completely. We spent a beautiful week together in Kuwait, making everyone aware that Freda's boyfriend was in town!

Julian gifted me a gold chain with a little ball at the end, which I still wear every day, nearly 46 years later! Ha! Ha!

In Kuwait, weekends were spent playing cards with friends. Each family would bring a dish, and we'd play through the night. The second time Julian visited, we taught him to play flush, and he won so much money he returned to Saudi Arabia first class! Before leaving, he told me he would tell his parents about us and his intention to marry me. I was over the moon!

When Julian left, I told my sister about his plans, and she advised me to write to him, saying I had no money and couldn't cook. Julian responded with, "Don't worry, we will live on Love and Fresh Air." Ha! Ha!

My brother-in-law Joe decided it was time to teach me how to cook. The next day, he took me into the kitchen and showed me how to cut a pomfret. Every day, he taught me different dishes. By then, I was working for Kuwait International Investment Company and doing well.

In December, I left Kuwait for Bombay to get engaged. Julian and I got engaged on December 28, 1977. We had a short time together, but it was enough for me to meet his family members and start dreaming about our future together.

Julian's Parents

Julian

Julian and his siblings

Chapter 9

The Wedding

Julian's parents were Francis and Lena Vaz. His dad, affectionately known as "Opa" by the grandchildren, was a talented drummer who played for the famous "Chic Chocolate Dance Band" and even for the film industry in Bombay. His mom, Lena, whom everyone called "Oma," had a passion for cooking, singing, and dancing.

Julian had three older sisters: Maxine, Justine, and Geraldine, who were collectively known as the "Ine Sisters" because of their shared love for singing. Maxine was a highly qualified professional working at the Reserve Bank of India. Geraldine held a prestigious position at Air India and even travelled to Germany to perform as an Indian dancer. Justine was a skilled seamstress who specialized in bridal gowns and also ran her own stitching classes.

Julian also had a younger brother, Franco, who was six years his junior and followed in their father's footsteps by playing drums for the film industry. Franco even acted in an Indian movie called "Andhadhun" and taught drumming to many students. Thirteen years younger than Julian was Patricia, affectionately known as Petu. Petu loved playing the piano and singing, and she also gave French lessons to students.

As Julian and I prepared for our wedding, we decided to share the expenses since my parents couldn't afford much. His parents helped us book the roof garden at MacRonell's in Bandra for the reception, the same place where all his three sisters had gotten married. Julian's parents were close friends with the owners, making it a special family tradition.

For the wedding invitations, I enlisted the help of Anita, my sister Jenny's best friend who worked in advertising. There was so much to do, but amidst all the preparations, my mother gave me a crucial reminder: "You better tell Julian to bring the visa with him when he comes down because

I am not going to let you get married if he cannot take you with him to Saudi Arabia." I trusted in miracles.

To ensure everything would work out, my mom took me to Mount Mary's Church in Bandra, where we prayed and lit candles, hoping Julian would secure the visa. Thankfully, he did! I decided to sing for our first dance, choosing "You're the Only World I Know" and went to several practices to get it just right. For our wedding car, we hired a beautiful powder blue Mercedes Benz.

The bridal party included Julian's brother Franco as the best man, my friend Jeroo as the bridesmaid, along with my sister Audrey and Julian's sister Petu. Maxine's son, John, was the page boy, and Justine's daughter, Maria, was the flower girl.

Finally, on January 7, 1978, we got married at St. Michael's Church in Mahim. About 500 guests attended our reception, including many musicians, which added to the festive atmosphere.

We spent our wedding night at the Hotel Centaur in Santa Cruz near the airport and flew to Goa early the next morning for our honeymoon. I was on cloud nine! We stayed at the luxurious Taj Hotel in Goa.

Our first morning in Goa, after breakfast, we decided to take a walk on the beach. To our surprise, we were the only ones dressed; everyone else, from grandfathers to grandchildren, was sunbathing in the nude! After our long walk, we returned to the hotel and I ordered a cocktail called a "Sinquerim special", made with the local drink Fenni mixed with pineapple juice. It was so delicious, and I was so thirsty that I gulped it down quickly. Before I knew it, I couldn't stand up. Ha! Ha! That was the first time I ever got drunk! Julian had a good laugh and ordered some snacks to help me sober up.

Our one-week honeymoon in Goa was wonderful, and on January 29, 1978, I flew back to Riyadh as Mrs. Freda Vaz.

Julian and I quickly settled into our new life together. His family welcomed me warmly, making me feel like I was always meant to be a part of their lives. Opa's stories of his days in the music industry and Oma's cooking made every visit special.

Julian's sisters were all incredibly talented and kind. Maxine, with her sharp intellect and calm demeanour, was always ready with advice. Geraldine's adventures as a dancer fascinated me, and Justine's creative skills inspired me. Franco, with his drumming and acting career, brought a lot of energy into the family, and Petu's musical talents added to the lively atmosphere of family gatherings.

Life in Riyadh was an adjustment, but Julian was my anchor. We enjoyed exploring the city together and finding little spots that reminded us of home. Our love grew stronger as we faced the challenges of settling into a new country.

I found a job at a local company, which helped me feel more integrated into the community. Julian and I made new friends and often hosted dinners at our home. These gatherings became a cherished tradition, filled with laughter, music, and good food.

In the midst of our busy lives, we always made time for each other. Julian's thoughtful gestures and unwavering support made me feel loved every single day. We dreamed of building a family together and creating a future filled with joy and adventure.

Our journey together was just beginning, and I couldn't wait to see what the future held. With Julian by my side, I felt ready to take on any challenge and embrace every opportunity that came our way. We were partners in every sense, sharing dreams, responsibilities, and an unbreakable bond.

As we navigated the ups and downs of life, our love remained constant. Julian's laughter, kindness, and strength were my guiding lights. Together, we built a life that was rich with love, filled with beautiful memories, and brimming with endless possibilities.

The Wedding

The Engagement

Our Wedding

Chapter 10

Julian and I returned to Riyadh where he was working for Areen Travels. His office was filled with a lively group of Palestinian boys, which made for an interesting work environment. Julian had rented a cozy one-bedroom apartment for us, and when we arrived, we were pleasantly surprised to find it fully decorated and furnished. The guys from his office had stocked the fridge with loads of food, provided all the cutlery and crockery we needed, and even gifted us a beautiful white carpet as a wedding present.

I now had to wear the Abbaya (Black cloak worn by Muslims). Thankfully I had to cover my head only in certain areas where there was a mosque. Julian came home one day and was furious with me because he got a complaint from the Muthawa (Priest) saying that his wife was in the balcony. Well, I went there to hang the clothes. I was only too happy not to go to the balcony again. One less job to do. Clearly the rules in Riyadh were very strict.

A few months into our new life, I found out I was pregnant. Unfortunately, three months later, I had a miscarriage and thankfully Justine stepped in and really took good care of me. I was very grateful to her.

It was a tough time, but we had each other for support. At that time, I was working for Bell Canada. On my birthday, Julian's Palestinian boss came over to wish me well and presented us with a beautiful music system. He also felt our one-bedroom apartment was too small and decided to book an entire building for the staff, moving us into a spacious two-bedroom apartment.

Julian and I, along with the manager and his wife, lived on the first floor, while the bachelors occupied the ground floor. Initially, it was challenging for me as I felt very lonely during the day when everyone was at work. I would often tell my mom, "I'm talking to myself, and soon the furniture might talk back to me." Ha! Ha!

One day, Julian came home with exciting news. One of his clients was selling an entire set of IKEA furniture for just 5,000 Saudi Riyals. This included a 350-liter Kelvinator fridge, a sofa set, a dining set, a crockery cupboard, a study table, a TV unit, bedside tables, and more. It was like a miracle!

Soon after, I started working for the World Bank. When I got pregnant again, complications arose, and I had to be on bed rest, leading me to give up my job. This pregnancy came with a lot of morning sickness. The Palestinian boys, Khalid & Talaat, were incredibly supportive, cooking amazing Arabic food for me. During this time, Julian had to go on a familiarization trip to Scandinavia. The guys took care of me, ensuring I had company and delicious food every evening. Strangely, I craved only Arabic food during this pregnancy.

Julian and I enjoyed watching movies at home, and one day we saw a show featuring Diahann Carroll with Sammy Davis Jr. And Telly Savales. I was so captivated by her name that I decided if we had a girl, we would name her Diahann-Carroll.

Julian always wanted a girl first. When it was time for my delivery, I went to Bombay, which was experiencing a severe drought at the time. There was no rain, and we were already in July. People were being told they might have to vacate Bombay if it didn't rain soon. In July 1979, my daughter was born at 1:32 in the morning, and miraculously, it started to rain and didn't stop for many days. Hence, we called her our "Rain Baby."

After the delivery, Julian asked the doctor if it was a boy or a girl. The doctor took a moment before answering, which worried Julian. Finally, the doctor announced, "It's a girl!" Julian was so excited that he hugged the doctor, who was confused because in India, people usually hope for a boy first. We named her Diahann-Carroll Vaz.

Julian gifted me a beautiful diamond pendant and chain after Diahann's birth. When Diahann was nine months old, Julian took us to London, where I did a lot of shopping for her at

Mothercare. We then went to Brussels for Julian's training. I would take Diahann in her pram to visit the malls in the morning, and in the evenings, Julian would take us out to explore the city. One day, while walking down the street, we passed a shop with nude women in the window. I thought they were mannequins until one of them waved at me! It gave me a good laugh.

We visited "The Grand Palace" in Brussels and met a South African gentleman who looked like Santa Claus. He was drinking beer from a huge mug, and Diahann grabbed it, enjoying sips from it. The gentleman was amused by how she kept pulling his hand for more. Ha! Ha!

When Diahann was two and a half years old, Julian and I went on a holiday to Singapore. Diahann, however, stayed in Bombay with Julian's parents. We stayed at the Hotel Sheraton and explored many sights. I was particularly impressed with how clean Singapore was; I even saw people shampooing the roads! We were warned that littering would result in a $100 fine. The Tiger Balm Gardens were beautiful, and the street food was excellent, though the shopping was quite expensive.

We celebrated our wedding anniversary on January 7th with a lunch at the Sheraton. After a day of sightseeing, I was exhausted and had my drinks too quickly, realizing I couldn't balance myself on the way to the buffet table. I made Julian walk behind me in case I fell! That was the second time I got drunk, and I learned my lesson—never drink fast after a tiring day!

Diahann was a very fussy eater, taking hours to eat anything. However, she was also very observant. One day, a friend came over, and she asked, "Mum, why is uncle wearing one black sock and one brown sock?" The guy was so embarrassed; he hadn't even noticed it himself. Ha! Ha!

Diahann loved talking on the phone. In those days, we didn't have mobiles, but even at four years old, she could identify callers trying to disguise their voices. She was also a very cranky baby, crying a lot, and I often struggled to figure out what was wrong. One day, during a lunch gathering, one of our friends bought her a beautiful Lyra crayon set and a large sheet of paper to colour on. From that day on, Diahann would spend hours colouring.

Being the first granddaughter, she was spoiled by all my sisters. She had gorgeous curly hair and was nicknamed "Curly Top." As she grew older, they started calling her "Halle Berry" because of her striking looks. Diahann loved dressing up and was always neat and tidy, helping me keep the house clean.

Diahann always had lovely birthday parties, with organized games and lots of prizes. Her friends eagerly awaited invitations to her parties. After her big 21st birthday bash, Diahann moved to Delhi to work at the call centre "GE Capital." She later became a voice and accent trainer. In 2007, she married Lino and moved to Dubai.

Diahann wrote a book, "Training the Prism," about her experiences in call centre training. In Dubai, she received an award for her second book, "Bree's Dreams," named after her daughter, Hannah Bree. She also founded the online luxury magazine "Glam/Amour," featuring everything luxurious.

In 2016, my eldest daughter Diahann gave birth to a baby girl. Julian and I went to Dubai for Hannah Bree's christening. It was my second trip to Dubai. They lived in the Sahara Towers, right across from the Sahara Mall. Every day, Julian and I visited Spinney's supermarket to bring home delicious Arabic dishes, reminiscing about our time in Saudi Arabia. We visited many places and did a lot of shopping in Dubai. The Dolphin show was particularly memorable.

Three years later, we returned to Dubai to celebrate Hannah Bree's 3rd birthday. Now eight years old, she is extremely talented, participating in various competitions and winning prizes. She is learning the piano and has already done a few recitals in Dubai. She even entered a worldwide online math competition. Hannah's love for drawing and painting makes us incredibly proud.

Life had come full circle in many ways, and our journey is filled with love, laughter, and countless memories. We are excited to see what the future holds for us and our growing family.

Diahann-Carroll

Diahann-Carroll

Chapter 11

Francis Leo

About three and a half years after Diahann's birth, I found myself pregnant again. This time, my belly grew so large that it caused quite a stir. On my flight to Mumbai, an air hostess worriedly told the captain that I looked like I might deliver on the plane. She eventually approached me and, to my surprise, recognized me from our hometown in Bombay. "Freda, can I have a look at your papers?" she asked. I reassured her, "Don't worry, I know the rules. My husband works in the airlines, and I'm only seven months along." She sighed with relief and laughed, admitting that the crew was worried because I was wearing an abaya and they thought I was a Saudi woman.

When I arrived in Bombay, my mother was shocked by my size, thinking I might be carrying twins. She insisted I get checked to confirm there was only one baby. Ha! Ha! My son was finally born in February 1983.

We named him after both our fathers: Francis Leo Vaz. He weighed 8 ½ pounds and measured 22 inches long. After the delivery, a lady in the hospital asked if I was still going to deliver. "No," I replied, "I already did." Even post-delivery, my stomach remained quite large. Julian was overjoyed with our son and gifted me a beautiful set of amethyst and coral jewellery.

Francis was a bundle of mischief right from the start. He kept everyone on their toes, especially his sister, Diahann. There was never a dull moment with him around. I had to be extra vigilant at birthday parties, as Francis had a knack for making a beeline for the cake. I often had to hold his hands to prevent him from diving in. During a desert picnic, all the cars suddenly stopped. One of the guys ran to our car and pleaded, "The cake is in your car, and Francis is there. Can we please take it away?" We all burst out laughing. His reputation for mischief was well-known.

Another time, we were in the car while Julian went into the post office. Suddenly, the car started moving backward—Francis had released the handbrake! We were all screaming in panic.

One of the most nerve-wracking incidents occurred at Saudi House, which was filled with delicate crystals. I was on the first floor buying cosmetics when Francis slipped from my hand and ran towards the crystals. I almost died of fright, imagining the sound of crashing glass. I quickly told Julian to grab him slowly. I was furious and gave him a stern scolding afterward.

At parties, I had to remind Francis not to eat too many nuts. Arab countries served a variety of nuts, and Diahann would always tease, "Mum, it's like a broken record. You tell him every time, and he still ends up vomiting on the way home." He simply loved to eat! One day, after collecting a gas cylinder, we suddenly smelled gas. Francis had opened the valve, and we all freaked out!

Despite his mischievousness, Francis was brilliant in his studies, earning excellent grades without much trouble. When Francis was in the

8th standard, I promised him a bicycle if he scored 90% in his exams. He scored 89.5%, and we jokingly told him he wouldn't get the bike. Upset, he went to his teacher and complained. The teacher assured him that his score was as good as 90%, so we bought him a bike.

Soon after, we received complaints about his reckless cycling. He cheekily remarked, "Mom, where do you think I get it from? Didn't you do the same, leaving the handlebars?" I had no reply to that!

Francis's love for science was evident, particularly chemistry. He graduated with distinctions in all six chemistry papers. He aspired to pursue forensic science, but it was too expensive for us to afford.

Francis had a beautiful singing voice. He secured second place at the "Kingfisher Competition" in Goa, singing "Kiss from a Rose" by Seal. He even recorded a single named "Spellbound," available on YouTube for listeners to enjoy. Eventually, he found his calling as an Event Manager and thrived in the bustling world of events. I often joked, "I can get the President of the United States faster than I can get my son! Ha! Ha!"

In 2013, Francis married Lizann, and they had a beautiful daughter, Dylan Madison Vaz. Dylan, our first granddaughter, inherited her father's and grandfather's height and charm but her gorgeous smile and loving personality are definitely from her mom!! From a young age, she loved posing for the camera, taking gorgeous photos. Now eight years old, Dylan excels in Taekwondo, swimming, and academics.

Watching Dylan grow up and witnessing her talents bloom brought immense joy and pride to our lives. Francis's journey from a mischievous boy to a successful event manager and loving father filled our hearts with happiness. Life continued to unfold with new adventures and cherished memories, each chapter richer than the last.

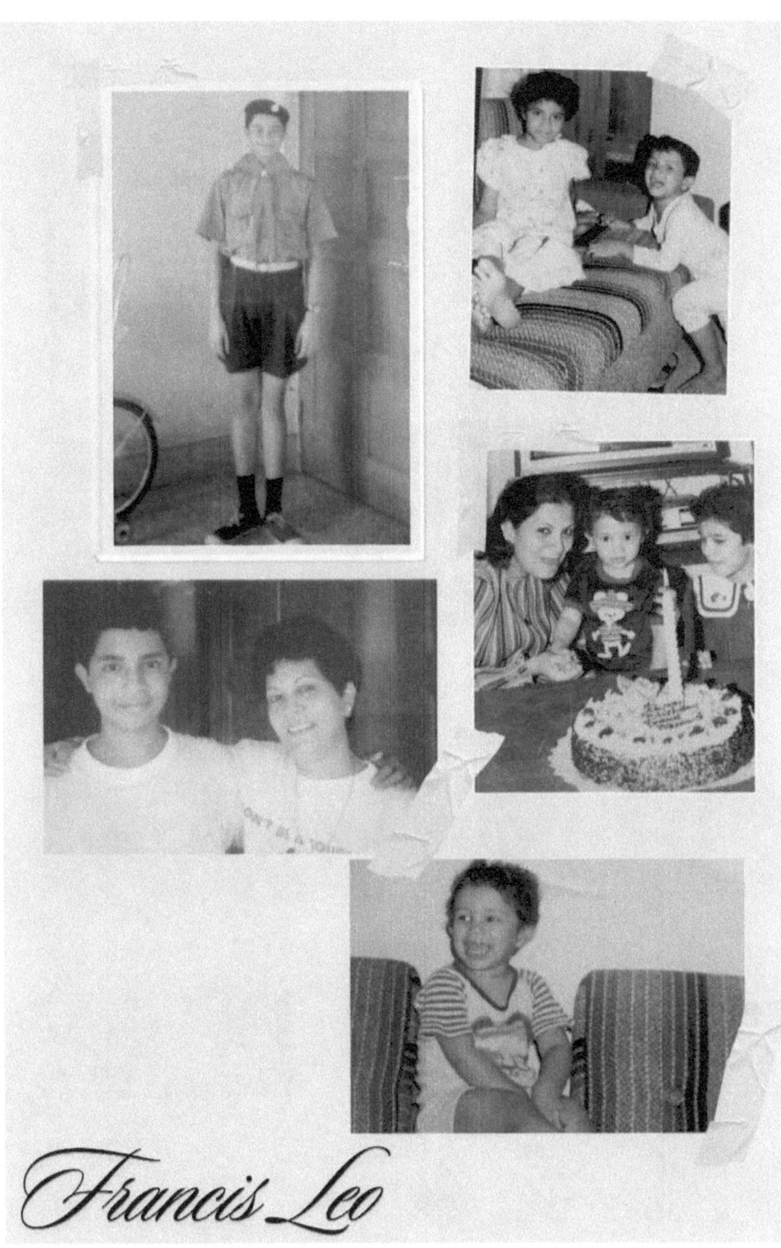

Francis Leo

Francis Leo

Chapter 12

Danielle

Six years after Francis was born, I found myself pregnant again. Around that time, I was hooked on a TV series featuring a beautiful little girl named Danielle. I didn't know the actress's real name, but I loved the name Danielle so much that I decided if I had a girl, that's what I'd call her. When I visited Bombay, my mother asked what name I had picked. "Danielle," I replied. She laughed and said, "What if it's a boy?" I quickly answered, "Then it will be Daniel." We both had a good laugh over that.

In September 1989, I went into labour. Julian had taken Diahann and Francis to the Bandra Fair for the Mount Carmel Feast. While they were having fun, I called and told them I was heading to the hospital. The kids were so upset because they were on the giant wheel and had to rush back. Diahann was thrilled, hoping for a girl, while Francis wanted a boy and wasn't too happy initially. But once he saw his baby sister Danielle, he was thrilled. Julian gave me a beautiful gold set to celebrate!

Friends would often tease, saying, "Why don't you get pregnant every year? Julian will keep giving you gold presents." Julian knew how much I loved jewellery, so his gifts were always thoughtful.

When Danielle was about four months old, Julian had to go for training in Jordan. He worked for Royal Jordanian Airlines and decided to take the whole family. Jordan was beautiful, but extremely cold. The kids loved the huge pizzas with buy-one-get-one-free offers. While there we visited a close friend, Talaat & his family for a meal. And though the meal in itself was amazing, the memory that stayed with us till today was how Talaat's mom kept feeding Francis, to the extent that he literally pleaded with me to make her stop! Francis ... the boy who loves to eat!

Unfortunately, Diahann caught chickenpox, so I had to return to Riyadh earlier with the kids while

Julian stayed behind. Eventually, Francis and I also got chickenpox. It was a terrible experience—burning with fever, Danielle still a baby, and Diahann, amazing as ever, took over the cooking and care. We were blessed to have Dr. Bonny visit daily to check on us.

Danielle's health was fragile. By age three, she had asthma and would often have severe attacks. We were constantly visiting doctors and hospitals for nebulization. She had no appetite and was very thin. Oma (Julian's Mum) would say, "Children with asthma usually grow up bent, but Danielle is growing tall and beautiful."

One day, on the way to primary school with Julian, Danielle saw cow dung on the road and said, "Dada, don't step in the dung, or I'll have to sing Happy Birthday to you." Ha! Ha! Another time, her classmates mistook Julian, who greyed early, for her grandpa. Annoyed, she asked him to stop coming to school and even wanted him to colour his hair! Today, people pay a lot of money for that beautiful grey hair!

Danielle was a beautiful and unique kid. She was left-handed like some of her cousins. When she was small, she loved joining fancy dress competitions in school. She won first place for 24carat gold where I joined 24 baby carrots around her neck, and she wore a gold dress.

She also won for dressing as a mermaid. That was hilarious because she had a problem moving with her outfit, but she did a good job.

Danielle also won a prize for the Badam tree. She got second place for The Black Cat. Her brother Francis composed a poem for her. I made her wear a black shirt and pant and a red velvet collar with black pearls in it. Unfortunately, she forgot her lines and won second place, but her brother was furious with her after all the trouble he took to write the poem. Ha! ha!

As she grew older, she joined Judo classes. At home she loved eating fish unlike her other two siblings. She would make sure it was stripped to the bone. I used to always tell her that I would find a fisherman's son for her.

Danielle and Francis got along very well. They used to play cricket in the house which used to get my blood pressure up. She was like a tomboy who went to play with all her brothers' friends.

When she grew up in her twenties, she went into modelling. She had sexy' long legs! Every time I stood in my balcony and saw the traffic moving slowly, I knew Danielle was at the bottom of the building. When she came home, I would say "Why you causing so much traffic jam outside? We don't need any accidents! Then she would scream "Mama, stop it"! Ha! Ha!

She always loved to sit with me on the bike. Later she wanted to learn how to ride my bike but somehow failed. Finally, she got someone to teach her and then there was no turning back. She used to take me on the bike, and she would ride to work as well.

A memorable incident during the COVID-19 pandemic was when Danielle worked half-days. One afternoon, after her shift, she decided to take an internal road through fields on her bike. She spotted her dear Uncle Gratian, who had passed away years ago. Shouting "Hello, Uncle," she heard a reply, "Hello, Baby." Realizing her mistake, she sped home, spooked by the encounter.

Danielle missed a lot of school due to her health but managed to catch up each time. Her favourite subject was Maths. She did well in school and graduated in English Literature from St. Francis Xavier College, Mapusa.

Danielle did bartending in college and some modelling too as pocket money but had to stop after slipping and injuring her tailbone. She continued her bartending and delighted us with different cocktails on feast days. Eventually, she moved to Delhi and worked for a cosmetic company, where she learned professional makeup artistry skills. She later worked as a freelance hairstylist and makeup artist for brides.

When the wedding season was slow, Danielle made delicious chocolates with various Flavors like rum and raisin, hazelnut, whiskey shooters, masala chai, fruit and nut, marzipan, drunken monkey, chocolate crunch, and pista. Julian and

I helped with wrapping the chocolates, and I loved licking the pot when she was done! Ha! Ha!

Danielle landed a job with the Indian Soccer League (ISL) for 5 years in Goa as a makeup artist for the television anchors. She did the make up for football players for their photoshoots as well. She later joined as a Counter Manager for MAC Cosmetics Goa. She even assisted in handling the Online Reputation Management team for M.A.C Cosmetics India.

She would come home from work and entertain us with hilarious stories. She had a knack for making us laugh and would have made an excellent stand-up comedian. Whenever she irritated me, I'd say, "Stop chewing my brains!" She'd retort, "What brains? Diahann and Francis already chewed them. There's nothing left!" Ha! Ha! And then she'd joke, "Diahann and Francis gave you grey hairs; it's my job to colour them!" Ha! Ha! The house felt very quiet once she left.

Danielle married Oswald in 2023. He works in Macau as a graphic designer and has a passion for photography. They now live in Macau.

Life with Danielle brought us countless moments of joy, laughter, and love. Each chapter of her life, from her mischievous childhood to her successful career and marriage, added vibrant colours to our family tapestry. As I look back on these memories, I cherish the beautiful journey of raising such an incredible daughter.

For her wedding, Danielle had chosen a Bangle ceremony instead of the traditional Ross ceremony. Julian's sisters and nieces flew in from Bombay for the event, which was held at our home. They sang beautiful Konkani mandos while each family member placed bangles on Danielle's hand. We recorded the ceremony and shared it with friends. My childhood friend Pamela and her husband Nelson loved it so much that Pam suggested forming a small band to sing Konkani mandos at Ross ceremonies.

When Pamela first approached us with the idea of forming the Roceingers, I felt a wave of apprehension. The prospect of singing in Konkani, a language I didn't speak, seemed daunting. But deep down, I knew it was never too late to learn something new. I decided to embrace the challenge, determined to give it my best shot.

The journey began with intensive practice sessions, particularly focusing on the pronunciations. Every word and phrase needed to be perfect, and I spent countless hours practicing, listening, and repeating until they felt natural. Our group met for practice every Friday, and slowly but surely, I started to get the hang of it.

At first, the rehearsals were tough. I stumbled over words and often felt frustrated by my slow progress. But I was surrounded by supportive friends who encouraged me and helped me improve. Nelson would play the violin, Pamela the guitar, Julian the Gummot, with Sera & myself on vocals; and we all sing the mandos.

Over time, I began to enjoy the process. The melodies and rhythms of Konkani songs were beautiful, and I found myself getting lost in the music. The Roceingers became more than just a singing group; it was a community of friends bonded by our love for music and our commitment to overcoming challenges together.

Our performances started to improve as well. The more we practiced, the better we sounded. It was incredibly rewarding to see the progress we made as a group and to feel my own personal growth as a singer. I even started to look forward to our Friday practices, excited to see how much we could achieve together.

Reflecting on this journey, I realized that stepping out of my comfort zone and learning Konkani was a transformative experience. It taught me the value of persistence and the joy of embracing new challenges. Now, I can proudly say that I am pretty good at singing in Konkani. Ha! Ha!

This experience with the Roceingers reminded me of the importance of lifelong learning and the power of a supportive community. It showed me that with dedication and the right mindset, we can overcome any obstacle and achieve things we never thought possible.

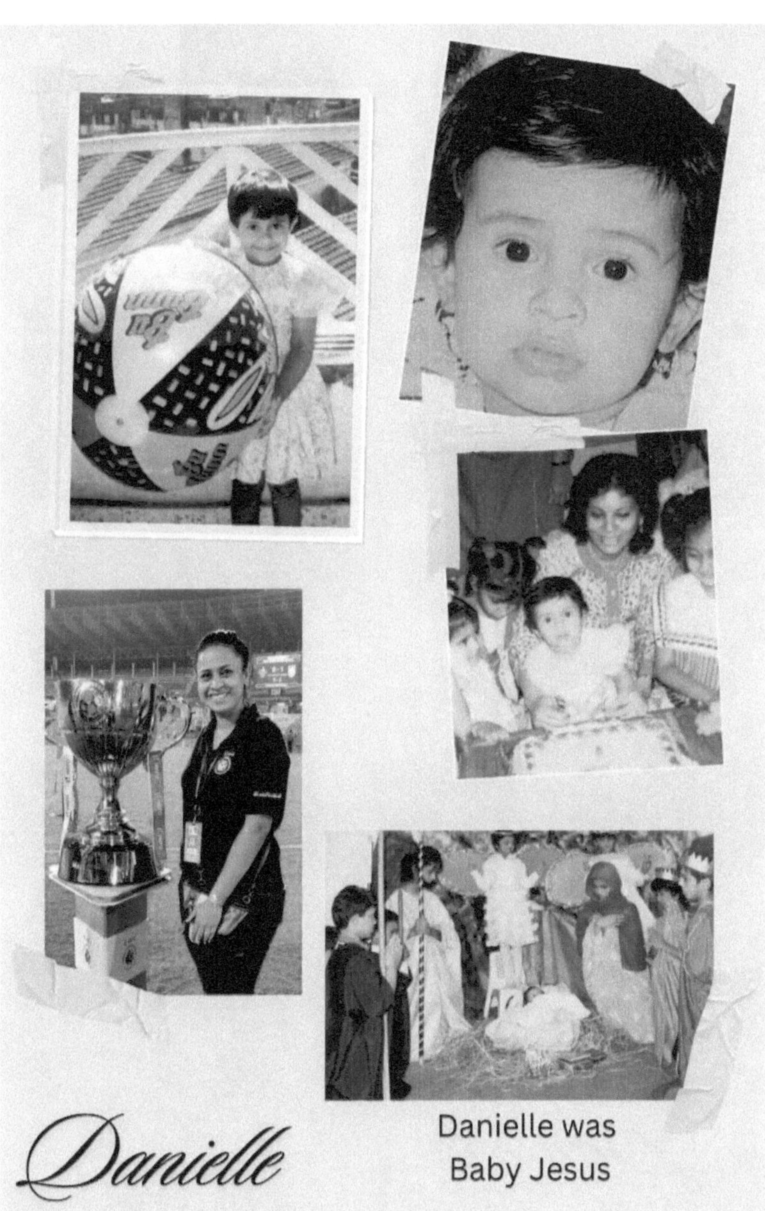

Danielle

Halloween
Make up

Danielle

My Kids

Chapter 13

Timeless Friendships

I want to share the story of our close friends, Henry and Mary Chu. Henry, originally from Pakistan, had Chinese parents, which made for an interesting blend of cultures. He spoke fluent Urdu, Hindi, and English. Appointed by the Bishop to have a Eucharistic service as a Lay Priest, Henry played a crucial role in our lives in Saudi Arabia. Since practicing any religion other than Islam was forbidden, there were no churches. Holy Communion had to be flown in from Dhahran, and Mass was held secretly in different homes. Many times, our home was the chosen spot, and after Mass, we'd have a communal dinner where each family brought a dish. Our local drink, "Siddiqui," was always a part of these gatherings.

Henry had a fantastic sense of humour and was an exceptional cook. He married Mary, a Filipina, and they had two children, Marie Chris and Timothy. Mary had a charming way of saying my name, "Fred..a," which always made me smile. When I was pregnant with Francis, I craved Filipino food, and Mary was more than happy to share her cuisine, even though she found our Indian food quite spicy. Henry, coming from a family of chefs, would often invite us over for meals.

Henry worked at a bank, and Mary had a job too. During this time, I helped out by babysitting their daughter, Marie Chris, along with our other Pakistani friend Roland Chandy's daughter, Christine. With my kids in school and me not working, this kept me busy and helped with our expenses. Henry and Mary became like family to us, and we enjoyed many memorable years together in Riyadh.

After Julian and I left Riyadh for Goa, Henry and Mary migrated to the USA. Sadly, Mary eventually passed away from cancer. Despite the distance and the years that have passed, Henry still calls us from the States, keeping our friendship alive.

Julian has his long-time friend Cyril, whom he knew from Bombay. Cyril was a crooner in a band, and I remember him from the Nine Pin stall when I sang for the Victoria Church Fete. He was also from Mahim and later came to Saudi Arabia. We had many parties with Cyril playing the guitar, and I was thrilled to have him accompany me during our singing sessions in Riyadh. I recall Cyril once telling me, "Freda, the first time you went out with Julian for a movie, he came to my house, and we drank and celebrated." It was a funny and touching memory. Cyril even named his son "Julian," and Julian and I are his godparents. Cyril and his wife, Norma, now reside in Calangute, Goa, and we continue to stay in touch.

Julian and I were fortunate to share a special bond with Dr. Bonny Pereira and his wife, Jenny. Dr. Bonny was an esteemed orthopaedic surgeon in Saudi Arabia, known for his exceptional skills and dedication. He was entrusted with the care of one of the Saudi princes and his family, but to us, he was much more than a doctor. He treated my family as if we were his own, offering care and support that went beyond professional duty.

One of the most memorable instances of his care was when Diahann contracted chickenpox. I had to return from Jordan with her while Julian stayed behind for his travel course. Soon after, Francis and I also caught the chickenpox. My case was severe, given my age at the time, and it was a full-blown attack. Dr. Bonny would visit us every morning to check our temperatures and overall condition. After his workday, he'd drop by again to see how we were holding up.

One night, my fever spiked alarmingly high. Dr. Bonny instructed me to call him at midnight to update him on my condition. Not wanting to disturb his rest, I waited until the morning. When I finally called, he was upset, saying, "I was waiting for your call." His concern was genuine, and his dedication to our well-being was unwavering.

There was a time when Diahann developed a strange pain in her arms and legs which made her very lethargic and unable to walk properly.

After conducting some tests, Dr. Bonny diagnosed that she had the GBS disease which at the time required extremely expensive medical treatment and a wide range of testing to establish the variant of GBS that she had contracted. Tests we did not have the finances to pay for. But we did what knew best and that was to put all our trust and faith in Dr. Bonny and his medical skills. After reviewing her case, he drew up a single treatment plan which he felt was the best financially and medically and told us to administer it to Diahann. We prayed that it was the correct medication for her strain of GBS, because if it wasn't the result was fatal.

10 days later, Diahann started showing promising results and eventually made a full recovery. A recovery we can only classify as a miracle, thanks to Dr. Bonny.

Another time, Francis had a severe bout of malaria, causing hallucinations. Dr. Bonny was there for us, managing Francis's treatment with the same care and precision.

And then when Danielle needed her appendix removed, he insisted on handling her treatment personally. His intervention and the intravenous injections he administered were pivotal in her recovery.

All three of my children held Dr. Bonny in the highest regard. They trusted that if they fell ill, he would make them well again. His diagnostic skills were unparalleled, and his compassion made a lasting impact on our family.

Julian and Dr. Bonny shared a deep friendship. Dr. Bonny had a love for singing and cooking, talents that added joy to our gatherings. We spent many wonderful times together at parties, where his presence was always a delight. Jenny and I also shared a close bond. We could spend hours talking on the phone, discussing everything from our children's school lessons to upcoming social events. Our sons were classmates at the Indian Embassy School in Riyadh, which further strengthened our connection.

In 2020, during the height of the COVID-19 pandemic, Dr. Bonny fell ill. His condition worsened, and he passed away on May 27th. Our entire family was heartbroken. Due to COVID-19 restrictions, we couldn't attend his funeral. Watching the online mass, we were filled with sorrow, and many tears were shed. His passing left a significant void in our lives. Even now, we feel his absence deeply and miss him terribly.

Dr. Bonny's legacy lives on in our memories, a testament to the profound impact one person can have on the lives of others through kindness, care, and unwavering support.

Julian & Cyril

Henry, Mary Chu with Marichris
and Timothy

Khalid & Talaat

Cyril & Henry with Francis

Dr. Bonny Pereira
& Danielle

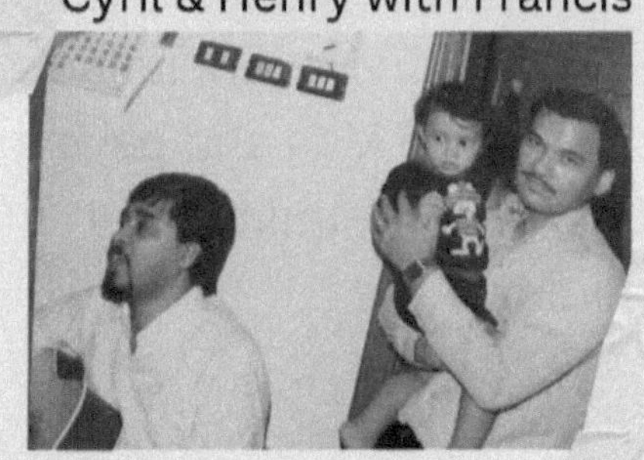

Friends Forever

Chapter 14

New Beginnings: Unexpected Ventures

In 1983, when our son Francis was born, Julian and I decided to find a place in Goa where we could eventually settle down, away from the hustle and bustle of Bombay. We found a building under construction and booked a three-bedroom flat before heading back to Saudi Arabia. Each month, we diligently sent the instalments for our future home. But soon, the Saudi government imposed a rule that restricted women from working unless they were teachers or worked in banks. This new policy meant we had to survive on Julian's single salary while raising two kids and paying for the flat in Goa. It felt overwhelming, but I always believed in miracles.

A friend of ours, a Parsi lady, approached me with an interesting opportunity. She knew a British woman who owned a video library and wanted to sell her entire collection of 100 movies for 5,000 riyals before returning to London. The money was beyond our reach, but our friend offered to lend it to me. My father had always been strict about borrowing money, insisting that if you couldn't afford something, you shouldn't buy it. Despite my hesitation, my friend's persistence convinced me to take the loan.

Once I acquired the collection, I faced the daunting task of paying back the money. Inspiration struck when I decided to sell all the children's movies. I distributed flyers in supermarkets and, within a week, sold 50 tapes, returning half of the loan. With the remaining tapes, I started my private video library. I created a list of movies, and clients would call to rent them. The deal was to rent out seven movies for the week. Julian helped me deliver the tapes, and the business flourished. Soon, I was able to repay the loan and reinvest in the business by converting the Betamax tapes to VHS, expanding my clientele further. I even sold the old Betamax tapes and bought a Commodore computer, enhancing my business operations. An Indian friend from the American Embassy supplied us with the latest movies, making our collection even more appealing.

Life in Riyadh was vibrant despite the strict environment. We organized many parties, but the Christmas parties were legendary. They were known as "The Party of the Year," complete with invitation cards, games for kids and adults, carol singing booklets, and a feast that took three days to prepare. We also had local alcohol called Siddiqui, adding to the festive spirit. One Christmas, we even had a live crib with Diahann as Mother Mary, Francis as a shepherd boy, and baby Danielle, only six months old, as Baby Jesus.

Trip to Jordan

Christmas Carol
Party

Gulf Life

Entering Riyadh house
as Mr And Mrs Vaz

First visit to Kuwait

Riyadh Gang

Chapter 15

Arriving Goa

In 1990, during the kids' holidays in Bombay, news broke about the Gulf War. We hurried back to Saudi Arabia, packed our belongings into a container, celebrated Danielle's first birthday, and flew back to Bombay, leaving Julian behind. It was challenging with a one-year-old, a six-year-old, and an eleven-year-old. Especially dealing with customs in Bombay and transferring our things to Goa. Fortunately, our flat was ready, providing us with a much-needed home base.

My sister Jenny and my son helped me set up the flat in Goa. Despite my lack of experience in assembling furniture, Francis, only six and a half, managed to put our double bed together, impressing me with his observation skills. He said, "No problem, Mom, I saw Dada using the Allen key to dismantle the bed." I was shocked that he was so observant at 6.5 yrs. of age. He managed to fix the double bed perfectly so at least we had a bed to sleep on. He was really amazing! He was of great help with all the chores in the house, opening boxes etc. After a week, we returned to Bombay, only to come back to Goa with all 3 kids on November 30, 1990.

Settling into Goa was a new challenge. I had to secure school admissions for Diahann and Francis, set up utility connections, open bank accounts, and do groceries. Our flat on the third floor with 79 steps became a daily workout. I often ran up and down the stairs, singing or whistling, drawing curious looks from the locals. Despite the physical strain, I believed in miracles and drew strength from my faith.

One day as I was returning from the market a friend of ours, who also came down from Kuwait, saw me and was wondering what I was doing in Mapusa. I told him I live here now and I was having a problem getting an electrician.

Every day the shopkeeper said "Falian" which means tomorrow in Konkani. That was the first Konkani word I learnt. Fortunately, this guy came the next day with his Black & Decker drilling machine and fixed all the curtains, fans and TV etc. The kids were thrilled since now they could watch some TV. He was such a blessing to us because every time I needed help, he was there to help me.

When the container with our belongings arrived in Bombay, I headed to customs to sort everything out. There, I unexpectedly ran into old friends from Kuwait, Mr. Joe Lobo and his wife, Joyce. I had first met them back in Kuwait and discovered that Joe's sister was actually related to me on my father's side. It was quite a pleasant surprise, and we quickly caught up on life.

Joe and Joyce were also in the process of settling down in Goa. They had a beautiful home in Parra that looked like a pagoda, quite close to my Granny's place. Joyce and I became very close friends. I would visit them frequently, enjoying their company and their wonderful sense of humor. Joyce was a retired teacher from Bombay, and both she and Joe had an infectious zest for life. Whenever Julian and I needed advice, we knew we could count on them.

Sadly, our time with Joe was cut short. He suffered a heart attack and passed away. After Joe's death, Joyce started spending her time shuttling between Goa and Dubai, where her daughter Jill lived. The loss of Joe was hard on all of us, but Joyce remained a pillar of strength. However, life had another blow in store for us when Joyce too passed away. Her absence left a void in my life, and I deeply missed our heartfelt chats.

Despite the sorrow, there were also many moments of joy and laughter during those years. Danielle, my daughter, became very close to Joyce's granddaughters, who visited from Dubai every July and August. Joyce had a playful spirit, and she loved teasing and entertaining Danielle.

One memorable afternoon, Joyce bought a flower pot shaped like a frog, inspired by the fairytales that Danielle and her granddaughters often read together. One evening, while the adults were having tea in the garden, Joyce noticed Danielle staring at the frog-shaped pot. With a mischievous grin, Joyce said, "Baby, maybe if you kiss the frog, it will turn into a prince." Danielle, who was going through a phase of believing in fairytales, was completely grossed out by the idea. She looked up at Joyce, wrinkled her nose, and quickly responded, "NO, THANK YOU!"

Joyce giggled and walked back into the house, leaving her granddaughters in fits of laughter at Danielle's reaction. It was these small moments of joy and connection that made our time together so special. Even though Joyce and Joe are no longer with us, their memory lives on through the laughter and love they brought into our lives.

Reflecting on those days, I realize how blessed we were to have friends like Joe and Joyce. They were more than just friends; they were family. Their kindness, humor, and wisdom left an indelible mark on our lives. And even in their absence, the stories and memories we shared continue to bring a smile to my face.

We were fortunate to have wonderful neighbours, particularly Simon and Leoney Pereira. They were a devout couple with a fantastic sense of humor. Every day, I would take Danielle in her pram to drop Francis off at St. Francis Xavier School, a good 15-minute walk from our house. Leoney noticed my daily routine and insisted that I leave Danielle in her care. Before long, Danielle was spending a lot of time at their house, and we would teasingly call her half Pereira. Ha! Ha!

Simon and Leoney had two sons at the time, both attending St. Britto's School. Our families became very close, sharing many moments and meals together. Leoney was famous for her amazing potato chops, which we all relished. She was always there for me whenever I was sick, offering her help and companionship since they lived right next door.

Simon played a crucial role in teaching Julian how to ride our Bajaj Chetak bike. He even helped Julian bring the new bike all the way from Vasco. Their sons grew up well, one eventually marrying and settling in Canada, while the other chose a life of service and became a priest.

Julian would always tease Simon and Leoney, calling them the best neighbours in the whole world. Our bond with the Pereira family was more than just neighbourly; it was like having an extended family right next door. The warmth and support we shared with them made our everyday lives richer and more enjoyable.

In school, Francis became close friends with a girl named Diana. Her mother, Cheryl, a former nurse, and I became good friends. Cheryl was a fantastic cook and a great support when my kids fell sick. Our friendship deepened over shared problems and countless hours on the phone. Sadly, Cheryl passed away from cancer, leaving a void in my life.

In February 1991, Julian left his job and joined us in Goa, much to the kids' delight. He found work at a travel agency in Panjim and later with Jet Airways, Sahara Airlines, and finally as a Travel Manager for TCI (Travel Corporation of India). Being part of the TTAG (Travel and Tourism

Association of Goa), we used to attend the annual functions on July 4th, sponsored by different hotels. These events were family-friendly, with games for the children, prizes, and lavish dinners. The Vaz family often won hotel stays, turning these occasions into much-anticipated events.

∞∞∞∞∞∞∞∞∞∞∞∞∞∞∞∞∞∞∞∞∞∞∞∞∞∞∞∞∞∞∞∞

Reminiscing on the different stories of the three kids, I must mention about our Dining Table (which we had in Saudi Arabia), which came along with the other furniture. It changed three houses in Riyadh till we finally settled in Goa. It has been almost 45 yrs. old, and it is still with us. If this table could talk, it would speak volumes about my kids!

Julian and I had a rule from the time the kids were small, that if ever they had a problem, we would all sit at the table and discuss it. We had an excellent relationship with the kids. They always had the habit of confiding in us for everything. We are so blessed!

Julian always told the kids, "Remember this house is in your mother's name, so if you want to get married, first make sure you have the money, then choose your partner and we will come to your wedding and give you a wedding gift."

Well, Julian and I got married with our own money, so we made sure the kids were not looking in our direction to get them married. Ha! Ha! Fortunately, all three kids paid for their own weddings, and we are so proud of them!

I remember telling one of Danielle's friends' mothers about how we bring up the kids and how we told them that they have to pay for their own wedding. One day this same lady came up to me and said, "Freda I heard Diahann is getting married, Does the rule still apply?" I said "YES" definitely. She was shocked! She thought I was only joking.

As a child, Diahann took ages to eat her food and used to sit on one side of the table while Francis sat on the other end. It was like North and South Pole. I had to say, "Diahann eat fast, and Francis eat slowly and chew your food". It was a daily affair. Ha! Ha!

Diahann had a habit of keeping prawns at the edge of her plate so she could enjoy it after all her food was over. But every time she looked away to talk to someone, Francis would grab a prawn and shove it in his mouth. He was faster than the average bear!

Another hilarious incident that took place at the dining table was when Diahann hated to drink milk and Francis loved milk. Every evening at teatime I would place a cup of milk in front of them and by the time I turned to go to the kitchen to get my tea, Francis has not only gulped his milk but has finished Diahann's too! He was smart enough to leave a little at the bottom of the cup to show that Diahann drank the milk.

Julian used to keep a jug of cold water to have after his lunch and one day Diahann knocked down the jug by mistake, and before she knew it, she was screaming because she had cold water all over her lap. Ha! Ha!

Julian loved eating one green chilly with his food and Francis and Danielle used to take turns to pick out the hottest chilly. Invariably, the moment Julian took the first bite, he used to start getting hiccups. Everyone used to have a good laugh. That meant that the person who chose it, did a good job of selecting!

During exam days, I used to wake up the kids at 5.00am to go through their lessons before they went for the exam. Most of the time when I entered the dining room, I would find Diahann fast asleep at the table. Then they got smart, the moment they heard the ball chain which used to make a sound when I entered, they would pretend to study. So, I got even smarter! I used to creep up on them by holding the chain in my hand and they used to literally jump out of their skin!

Not to forget the times when they went around and around the table to avoid getting whacked by me. Ha! Ha! It used to bring back memories of my childhood days!!

Another hilarious incident involved Diahann and Francis arguing over a piece of paper that tracked who had last licked the tongue roast pot. Their heated debate, full of accusations, ended with both of them storming into the kitchen to find me laughing at their seriousness. It's moments like these that remind me of the joy and chaos of raising three unique children.

The table can extend on both sides, so during parties in Riyadh and in Goa for the children's birthdays, it used to be full of good food.

As the kids slowly grew up and left the house to get married, whenever they used to come over with their spouses, we used to talk and tell their spouses all the fun we had at this table.

Our home in Goa became the backdrop for many family stories, especially around our dining table, which had travelled with us from Saudi Arabia. It had seen countless meals, discussions, and celebrations.

Diahann, our eldest, was neat and organized, often accused of having OCD. She always knew where everything was, and her computer skills were a great help, especially with my club posters. Francis, on the other hand, was more chaotic, his cupboard often looking like a cyclone had hit it. Cleaning his room periodically became a necessity, much to his dismay. Danielle loved online shopping, her parcels arriving regularly. Her cupboard was full of neatly organized boxes, each with its specific purpose. Her passion for fashion and jewellery was evident, and she had a knack for creating funny reels on her phone.

Life in Goa was a mix of new challenges and cherished moments. From the daily routines to special occasions, our journey was a testament to resilience, love, and the belief in miracles. Through it all, our dining table remained a symbol of family unity, witnessing our laughter, arguments, and shared meals. As our children grew and moved on, they carried with them the values and memories we created in our little home in Goa.

Nelson, Pamela & Sera
-The Roceingers

Cheryl Almeida

Simon & Leoney

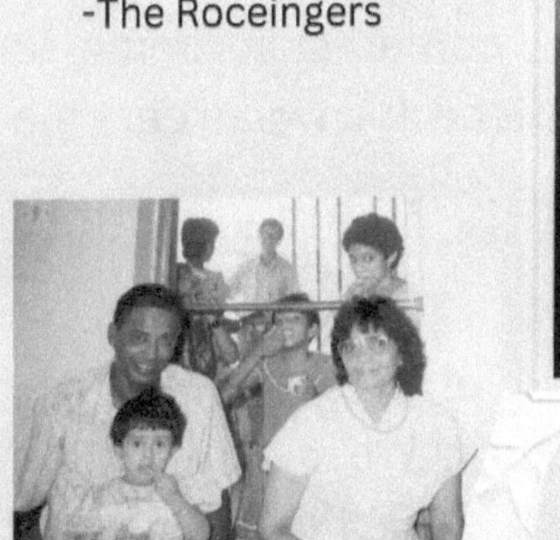

Joe & Joyce Lobo

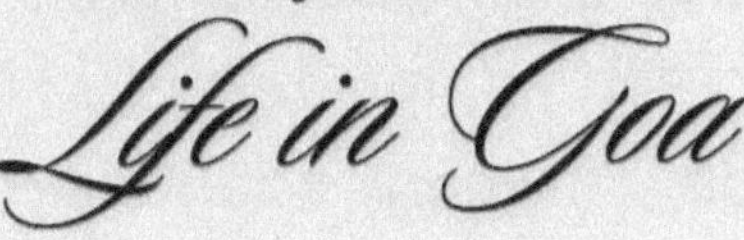

Life in Goa

Chapter 16

Regal Circulating Library

Julian had always been keen on trying new ventures, and one day he came up with an idea that excited us both. He had purchased a small 12 square meter shop at the bottom of our building, and we decided to turn it into a library. This would allow me to stay close to home while running the business. We envisioned a cozy spot where people could come and immerse themselves in books, a place that would become a local favourite.

We began by stocking up on a variety of novels and comics from Bombay. We registered the shop as "Regal Circulating Library," with high hopes that it would draw in book lovers from our community. Francis, always eager to help, took on the task of drilling and setting up shelves for our growing collection. Julian spent countless hours meticulously covering the books to protect them from wear and tear.

Initially, the library seemed like a promising venture. We had a good mix of genres and a wide selection of comics that we thought would appeal to the younger generation. We rented out novels and comics, waiting eagerly to see the library bustling with readers. However, we soon discovered that times had changed. The new generation was not as interested in reading as we had hoped. While the comics were popular, the novels remained largely untouched on the shelves.

Realizing that the library was not going to be the success we had envisioned, we decided to adapt. The novels, which were gathering dust, needed a new purpose. We contacted the nearest schools and offered to sell the books to them at a discounted rate. The schools were happy to take them, and at least we knew the books would be put to good use.

Despite our efforts, the library didn't last long. After about a year, we decided to close it down. It was a bittersweet moment; we had poured our hearts into creating a space that we thought would thrive, but the reality was different. Yet, we learned valuable lessons from this experience. It taught us about the changing interests of the younger generation and the importance of adaptability in business.

Although the library didn't turn out to be the bustling hub we had imagined, it brought our family together in a new way. Francis learned new skills, Julian and I spent quality time working on the project, and we all shared the ups and downs of running a small business. This chapter of our lives, while short-lived, was filled with effort, creativity, and family bonding.

Chapter 17

Seconds To Go

One day, I looked around our three-bedroom flat and realized we had accumulated a lot of unnecessary stuff from our time in Saudi Arabia. The excess clutter was overwhelming, and it was clear we needed to downsize. I decided to put the word out that I was selling some foreign goods. To my surprise, within a week, everything was sold out. People even started coming to the house, asking if I was selling the items inside as well. I explained that we had just moved in from Saudi Arabia and were trying to settle down.

During that time, the Gulf War had caused many people to relocate to Goa. When my friends heard about my successful sale, they begged me to sell their stuff too. That's when it struck me— this could be a brilliant business opportunity.

I registered the shop as "Seconds to Go" (a play on words suggesting both second-hand goods and the urgency of a last chance). It was a garage sale concept where people would give me their items to sell, adding a 10% commission for me. Every Saturday from 9:30 AM to 12:30 PM, I hosted a garage sale, and soon I had a waiting list of people wanting to sell their items. Imported goods were all the rage in Goa at that time, so the concept quickly gained popularity. Throughout the years, I had countless memorable and often hilarious moments running the shop.

The first consignment came from a close friend in Kuwait. I placed an ad in the newspapers: "Garage Sale at Seconds to Go, Shop No. 16." Believe it or not, there was a stampede in my 12-square-meter shop! People were pushing and shoving, making it incredibly difficult to manage. One man was eyeing a Black & Decker drilling machine and called his friend in Margao to ask if he should buy it. With so many people eyeing the same item, I had to tell him to decide quickly. Things were moving at a bionic speed.

Another memorable incident involved a couple from Delhi. The wife was interested in a green and white Chinese tea set, brand new and priced very reasonably. She wanted a discount, but I had to explain that the prices were set by the consignors and were non-negotiable. They left, and almost immediately, someone else bought the tea set. When the wife returned moments later, she was furious to find it sold, and her frustration was directed at her husband for not letting her buy it initially. Ha!

One time, a man came into the shop looking rather unassuming. I assumed he wouldn't be interested in or able to afford any of the brand new, imported items. Boy was I wrong! He bought a lot of stuff, paid in cash, and ended up being a regular customer every Saturday for the next 20 years. This taught me never to judge a book by its cover.

I had a poster in the shop that read, "You like, you buy. You no like, you no buy. Another man come, he like, he buy." It was a translation of an Arabic saying, and it always got a chuckle. Another poster read, "You break it, you bought it." Every

Saturday morning, there was a huge crowd waiting for me to open the shop.

Despite the success with most items, I struggled to sell clothes. Even though they were brand new and imported with tags, people just weren't interested. One day, two sisters asked me to sell their imported clothes. I warned them about my lack of success in that area, but they insisted, suggesting we could call it a "Ladies' Day Out." I decided to give it a try. I advertised in the newspapers and set up tables outside the shop with branded dresses, skirts, nighties, bras, panties, cosmetics, and jewellery. As predicted, people came, looked at the clothes, but bought other items instead. It remained a mystery to me why clothes wouldn't sell.

I have many incidents I'd love to share with my readers, some hilarious and others heartwarming. One day, an advocate from the building came storming towards me, asking where shop no. 16 was because people kept asking him about it. When I told him it was my shop and that I was running a garage sale, he was so fascinated that he and his wife started coming every Saturday.

Another funny incident involved a lady who would come every Saturday, telling her husband she was going to church. One of my regular customers bought a beautiful porcelain Nativity scene as a gift for her. She loved it and asked where he got it from. When he mentioned shop no. 16, she was speechless because she didn't want her husband to know she was a frequent visitor there. Ha!

One day, someone brought me a professional camera to sell. It was going for a surprisingly low price. A professional photographer came in, skeptical about the low price. After thorough inspection and a call to a friend, he finally bought it. The next week, a whole bunch of photographers came in, hoping for another deal like that. Ha! I told them I had no idea when I'd get another one.

The most unusual item I ever sold was a pair of skis. Who in Goa would need skis? But a customer bought them to display in his hotel. Wow! Who would've thought it?

I also sold a lot of antique furniture, from beds and lamps to carved bar tables. You might wonder how I managed to sell such large items in a small shop. I'd ask the consignors to provide photographs and details of the items, then advertise them. Interested buyers would come to the shop, and I'd arrange for them to view the items at the consignor's location. I sold entire housefuls of furniture, including appliances like A/Cs and washing machines.

One day, a guy came in with a lot of porcelain items from his closing shop in Calangute. He was moving and didn't mind selling them cheap. I contacted my regular customers who loved porcelain, and the items disappeared within hours. I was running short of space, so I hid some items on the top shelf, intending to display them the next Saturday. Regular customers spotted them, and everything was sold out before I knew it!

Word spread about the lady selling imported goods, and the Goa Chamber of Commerce wrote a huge article about me. I was the only lady in Goa running garage sales, and people wanted me to open shops in other locations. However, trusting someone else with consignors' items was out of the question. I also received write-ups in local newspapers like the Herald, Navhind Times, and Gomantak Times.

I had a rule that items could be kept in the shop for four Saturdays (one month). If they didn't sell, the consignors had to either reduce the price or take them back. Regulars knew this rule and would count the Saturdays, waiting for prices to drop. People would even stop by on Fridays, hoping to get first dibs on new items.

I kept a book with names and contact numbers of people looking for specific items. As soon as something came in, I'd call them, and they'd be there early on Saturday morning.

One day, a lady called to say she wanted to sell all the stuff she'd bought abroad. I explained the procedure, and she sent her driver with a friend. The elderly lady accompanying the driver was skeptical about the small shop's ability to attract customers. But when I opened the boxes, I found crystal decanters, glasses, and various crockery items, all in their original packaging. I was nervous about handling these delicate items in a crowded shop, so I called a few regular customers who loved crystals. They came immediately, and within an hour, almost everything was sold. Customers were even offering each other money to get certain items.

I called the lady to tell her most of the items were sold, and she was blown away. She sent two more consignments, and the same thing happened. Everything was sold out before Saturday.

Over the years, I started getting modern items like mobiles, laptops, music systems, and headphones, both second-hand and brand new. Someone even asked me to sell their wedding gown, but I declined, as clothes just didn't sell in my shop.

Eventually, I started getting consignments from locals, including their wedding presents. People would come to the shop to buy gifts for birthdays or weddings.

Looking back, "Seconds to Go" became more than just a shop. It was a community hub where stories were shared, laughs were had, and treasures were found. I learned so much about people, business, and the importance of adaptability. Even though it started as a simple garage sale, it turned into a beloved part of many lives in Goa.

Seconds To Go

Goa Talent Seekers - Talent Touchdown

Business Minded

Chapter 18

Goa Talent Seekers

– Talent Touchdown

As the years rolled by, my business started to slow down. The supply of imported goods dwindled, and I had fewer items to sell. That's when a new idea struck me—something that could bring joy to the community, especially the children. This is how "The Goa Talent Seekers" was born.

I gathered a few friends and formed a committee. We registered the non-profit organization and set out on a mission to uncover and showcase the hidden talents of Goa's youth. I spread the word through newspapers and local schools, announcing our search for talented kids. We received an overwhelming response, with over 200 children registering from all corners of Goa. Each child provided their name, contact number, and the category they wanted to audition for. We had various categories: singing in multiple languages, dancing, magic, compering, instrumentals, mimicry, and more.

We booked St. Mary's School Hall for three days of auditions. Each day was dedicated to a different category, and we had judges for every talent. From the multitude of talented children, we selected the top 50 for our first show. It was a six-month project. Every afternoon, we held practice sessions at my house. I coached the singers, Julian trained the comperes, and we hired a choreographer for the dancers. Those selected for Indian dancing practiced with their teachers, while kids playing instruments like piano, guitar, violin, and tabla prepared on their own.

Meanwhile, Julian and I spent our evenings seeking sponsors. It was challenging as many companies weren't interested in sponsoring a children's show. We also avoided tobacco and alcohol companies for obvious reasons. Thankfully, we received significant support from family and friends abroad, enabling us to run the program without charging the kids. The parents were thrilled, and whenever I called for a practice session, the excitement in their voices was palpable. The kids eagerly attended practices, and no one wanted to leave when the sessions ended.

Our first show, "Talent Touch Down," was scheduled for April 15, 2001, at the grandest venue in Goa: Kala Academy in Panjim. As we neared the event date, we visited an orphanage to identify their needs. We made a list of items like books, colour pencils, erasers, pillows, buckets, and blankets. Instead of having a famous chief guest, we invited the orphan children to the show, seating them in the front row.

The participants sold tickets to cover expenses, which included renting the hall for ₹10,000 for a four-hour program and hiring the sound guy for ₹5,000. We were fortunate to secure sponsors who donated items for the children. Each participant received a backpack filled with goodies like crayons and perfumes, plus an envelope with ₹100. We also gave away prizes like dinners and hotel stays for lucky ticket holders, making the audience very happy.

The highlight of the show was when our participants presented gifts to the orphans on stage. I had told the kids, "We are recognizing your talent and giving you an opportunity to develop your self-confidence on a large platform. In return, we must help the orphans." This touching moment brought tears to the eyes of the audience.

The participants were transported by bus, and sponsors provided them with pizzas, ice creams, hamburgers, and more. The kids were well taken care of and were thrilled to be part of the event. After the show, parents praised the positive impact it had on their children's lives. Their confidence had soared, and they were now recognized and invited to perform at their school programs.

Soon, we began preparing for the next show. The second show was held on November 18, 2001, close to Children's Day on November 14. We distributed chocolates to everyone in the audience, and it was another huge success. It was amazing to see young kids perform magic and mimicry. Our third show took place on November 30, 2002. Unfortunately, we couldn't continue with more shows due to a lack of sponsors. Still, I was proud to have made 150 children happy.

One memorable incident happened a few years later. I was approached to provide some kids to perform at an event. When I asked a group of dancers, they replied, "You'll have to ask our manager!" I was thrilled to see how far they had come. Today, those kids are all doing well, and most are now married.

Reflecting on this journey, I realized that "The Goa Talent Seekers" had not only brought joy to children but had also enriched my life with unforgettable memories. The excitement, the laughter, the practice sessions, and the shows were all experiences that shaped the lives of everyone involved. It was a beautiful chapter in my life, filled with growth, learning, and the satisfaction of making a positive impact on young lives.

Chapter 19

Rediscovering Life after Retirement

In 2006, Julian retired from his role as Manager at the Travel Corporation of India (TCI). To celebrate this new chapter in our lives, we decided to take a much-needed holiday to Bangkok in August. It was the first time in many years that we went on vacation just the two of us, and the experience was truly enjoyable.

Bangkok greeted us with its vibrant energy and beautiful sights. Our first stop was the famous Indra Market, a bustling hub of activity where we could shop for almost anything. We wandered through the maze of stalls, marvelling at the variety of goods on display. From there, we embarked on a city tour, eager to see all the must-visit attractions Bangkok had to offer.

One of the highlights of our trip was the visit to the Gem Factory. We were fascinated by the intricate process of jewellery making and ended up purchasing some exquisite pieces. The craftsmanship was impeccable, and the gems sparkled brilliantly under the showroom lights. It was a treat to bring back something tangible from our travels.

Bangkok's street food was another delightful discovery. We savoured the flavours of local delicacies, from spicy noodles to sweet desserts. Each bite was an adventure in itself, and we made sure to try as many different dishes as possible. The bustling food stalls were always crowded, a testament to the delicious offerings available.

A visit to the Temple of the Emerald Buddha left us in awe. The temple's intricate architecture and the serene beauty of the Emerald Buddha were truly captivating. We spent hours exploring the temple grounds, taking in the spiritual ambiance and admiring the detailed craftsmanship.

The flower market was another highlight of our trip. The vibrant colours and fragrant aromas of countless flowers were overwhelming in the best way possible. It was a feast for the senses, and we couldn't resist buying a few bouquets to brighten up our hotel room.

After long days of exploring, we treated ourselves to massages. Whether it was a full-body massage or just a relaxing leg massage, the experience was heavenly. We visited the Thai Massage School, where students practiced their skills under the watchful eyes of their instructors. It was fascinating to watch them work and even more wonderful to be on the receiving end of their expertise.

However, the trip wasn't without its challenges. I struggled to find a pair of shoes that would fit our son's big feet and finding clothes in my size proved to be difficult as well. Despite these minor inconveniences, our holiday in Bangkok was a memorable and rejuvenating experience.

Returning from Bangkok, we felt recharged and ready to embrace the next phase of our lives.

Julian's retirement marked the beginning of new adventures, and our trip was a reminder of the joys of exploring new places and spending quality time together.

This trip set the tone for our retirement years. We realized how important it was to take time for ourselves, to travel, and to experience new cultures. The memories we made in Bangkok were just the beginning of our journey into this exciting stage of life.

∞ ∞

In May 2013, Julian and I embarked on a deeply meaningful journey—a pilgrimage to the Holy Land. We boarded a Qatar Airways flight from Goa to Amman via Doha, filled with excitement and anticipation. Our pilgrimage took us across the King Hussein Bridge into Israel, where we began our exploration of the sacred sites.

Our first stop was Bethlehem, the birthplace of Jesus. Walking through the ancient streets and visiting the Church of the Nativity was a profoundly moving experience. From there, we journeyed to Tiberius, Nazareth, and Cana, each place steeped in history and spirituality. In Capernaum, we saw the remnants of what a bustling fishing village was once where Jesus performed many miracles.

One of the highlights was a serene boat trip on the Sea of Galilee. The peaceful waters and surrounding hills made it easy to imagine the biblical events that took place there. We visited the Church of Tabgha, known for the miracle of the loaves and fishes, and the Church of the Transfiguration on Mount Tabor, where Jesus is believed to have transformed before his disciples.

Our journey took us to the Mount of Temptations, Jericho Springs, and the Good Shepherd Church. In Jericho, we indulged in some shopping, picking up numerous souvenirs to bring home. We then visited the Dead Sea, where we couldn't resist taking a quick dip in its famously salty waters.

Jerusalem, the heart of our pilgrimage, was awe-inspiring. The old city held treasures of faith and history, from the Temple Mount and the Al-Aqsa Mosque to the Golden Gate. We prayed at the Western Wall, feeling the weight of centuries of devotion. At St. Anne's Church and the pool of Bethesda, we reflected on the miracles of healing attributed to Jesus.

Walking the Via Dolorosa, retracing the final steps of Jesus, was a deeply moving experience. We paused at each station of the cross, reflecting on his suffering and sacrifice. At Herod's Antonia Fortress, we tried to imagine the historical events that unfolded there. Standing in reverence at the Church of the Holy Sepulchre, the site of Jesus' crucifixion and resurrection, was the pinnacle of our pilgrimage.

From Jerusalem, we made our way to Sinai in Egypt, a long and arduous journey through the desert. The 162-kilometer bus ride took nearly three hours, but the landscape was breathtaking. In Sinai, we visited St. Catherine's

Monastery, nestled at the foot of Mount Sinai, where the burning bush is believed to have appeared to Moses. Aaron's tomb was another significant site that added to the spiritual depth of our journey.

Our pilgrimage then took us on a 416-kilometer bus ride to Cairo, which took approximately 12 hours due to numerous security stops. Despite the long journey, the sense of adventure and purpose kept our spirits high. In Cairo, we explored the Egyptian Museum, marvelling at the ancient artifacts and treasures of a bygone era.

We indulged in some shopping, particularly for Egyptian cotton clothes and perfumes, which were renowned for their quality. The Pyramids of Giza were an unforgettable sight, their grandeur and mystery leaving us in awe. That evening, we enjoyed a delightful Nile Cruise, taking in the city's lights and reflecting on the day's experiences.

Our exploration continued with visits to a Papyrus factory, where we learned about the ancient art of making paper, and the Coptic

Churches, which hold significant historical and religious importance. The Church of the Refuge of the Holy Family was particularly touching, as it is believed to have sheltered the Holy Family during their flight to Egypt.

After a memorable and spiritually enriching journey, we flew back to Goa from Cairo via Doha on Qatar Airways. The trip was beautifully organized, and every moment was filled with wonder and reverence. It was an experience that left a lasting imprint on our hearts and minds, deepening our faith and understanding of the sacred stories we had long cherished.

As we settled back into our routine in Goa, the memories of the Holy Land stayed with us, a constant source of inspiration and reflection. Our pilgrimage had not only brought us closer to our faith but also to each other, reminding us of the profound beauty and significance of the places we had visited. This journey was a testament to the enduring power of faith and the incredible history that connects us all.

Chapter 20

Sizzling Seniors Club

Turning 60 in March 2024 was a milestone that sparked a new idea in me. I thought, "Since I'm now a Senior Citizen, why not do something special for other seniors?" This inspiration felt like a divine nudge from the Holy Spirit. That's when I decided to organize a get-together exclusively for seniors.

I booked and paid for the St. Britto's School Hall, printed tickets, and gathered 60 seniors for a day of fun. With Julian's support, we arranged games, singing, and dancing. We also provided drinks and dinner for just ₹250 per person. The first party in April 2014 was a hit, thanks to the help from my kids, Francis and Danielle. The seniors enjoyed themselves so much that they immediately asked when the next party would be.

In August, I organized a "Rain Dance." A large group of ladies from South Goa even hired taxis to join the fun. The success of these events kept me motivated.

We also held a jumble sale where members showcased and sold their talents, like cooking, stitching, or crafting. Some brought plants, pickles, and snacks. After the sale, which was open to the public, we had a housie session. This event drew new members who were intrigued by the club.

We also had a "Game Nite" where we had tables for cards, carom, snakes and ladders, scrabble, Uno, tailing the donkey etc. All the members went down memory lane and they thoroughly enjoyed themselves. Some laughing, some cheating, and some learning new games. It was really an enjoyable evening.

Soon, the senior parties became a regular event every six months, but the seniors wanted more. They suggested starting a club. Initially unsure how to proceed, Julian and I, with help from friends, contacted the President of YMCA. In August 2019, we formed a committee and launched "The Sizzling Seniors Club."

Starting with around 90 members, we set the age requirement at 60-plus, though spouses could be younger. We printed forms and set an annual fee of ₹300 and a registration fee of ₹200. The committee included a President (me), Vice President (Julian), Secretary, Accountant, and groups for Entertainment and Catering. We met 15 days before each event to plan games, snacks, songs, quizzes, and housie. The club met on the last Sunday of every month, from 5:30 PM to 8:00 PM, each event featuring a different theme. My daughter-in-law, an amazing artist, created beautiful backdrops for our events.

One memorable event was a tea party where everyone brought a homemade snack on a quarter plate, with their ID number hidden underneath. We awarded a cash prize for the best snack and encouraged members to interact, exchange contacts, and win a prize for the most contacts. It was a fantastic way to foster new friendships.

Transportation became an issue for seniors traveling from distant places, especially at night. To address this, we shifted our events to the morning, starting with Mass at 9:30 AM and ending with lunch at 2:00 PM.

In February, we celebrated Valentine's Day and published our first souvenir. Members contributed compliments, articles, and paid advertisements from corporate sponsors, which brought in much-needed revenue. Despite the minimal fees charged to members, we needed funds for hall rental (graciously offered at a discount by the priests), cleaning, and miscellaneous expenses.

The Valentine's Bash was a highlight, with a stunning backdrop created by Lizann, my daughter-in-law. We hired a compere and bartender, offering free alcohol to all members.

The games were hilarious, and spirits were high! One game, the Tag Dance, involved cardboard cutouts of a male and female in bikinis with tassels of lucky numbers. Watching seniors grab these cutouts and chase each other around the hall was a riot. Everyone had a great time, and the event ended with each member receiving a chocolate heart giveaway.

Sadly, the COVID-19 lockdown in March 2020 halted our events. Many members contracted the virus, and we were deeply worried. Julian and I also tested positive and were isolated for 14 days. Our daughter Danielle took excellent care of us, ensuring we did exercises to stay fit despite our weakness. We were especially concerned for Danielle, who has asthma, but she remained healthy and diligently sanitized our living space daily. Her dedication was a blessing.

During this tough time, kind-hearted people provided us with free food. It took a while for me to regain my energy, especially since we also faced cyclonic winds that flooded our balcony. Danielle managed everything on her own. We lost many good friends during this period.

We held an online Mass in February 2021 and finally met in person again in August 2021 for our 2nd Anniversary Mass at Britto's. As soon as the lockdown lifted, we organized an overnight trip to Pedro Arrupe in Raia, South Goa. We arranged a bus to pick up all the members from Mapusa, leaving at 8:30 AM and arriving at 11:00 AM. Everyone enjoyed the beautiful property with its fruit and flower trees and the stunning chapel with glass windows showcasing the greenery outside. The Jesuit priests provided insightful talks, and we had plenty of entertainment and delicious food. The members loved the morning walks on the hills in the refreshing cool weather.

We also hosted a First Aid talk for the seniors, which was very informative. Everyone was surprised by the various ways seniors could avoid accidents in old age.

Our committee is amazing, always coming up with fantastic games. It's heartwarming to see seniors enjoying themselves and dancing so well. Thanks to a special sponsor, we could provide free drinks twice a year, once for the anniversary and again for the Christmas Bash.

For our Christmas Bash, one of the members dressed as Santa and distributed small gifts. We also had a carol singing session and gave blind-out numerous prizes, including lucky ID, lucky dancing couples, and spot prizes. Sponsors generously provided gift vouchers, ensuring almost everyone went home with a prize. After a few drinks, the atmosphere was electric, and the buffet lunch, featuring dishes like sorpotel, sannas, and vindaloo, was a highlight.

During the Christmas Bash, we surprised members over 80 years old with FREE LIFETIME membership cards. Many members turning 80 this year will receive this benefit, provided they complete one full year with the club.

Membership is slowly increasing, now approaching 140. The membership fee has risen to ₹600 per year, with a registration fee of ₹200. We charge ₹200 per person for lunch, and sometimes members sponsor lunch, snacks, or desserts. This financial support helps cover monthly expenses as the cost of living rises. Members often wonder how we manage the club, and I always say, "I believe in miracles!"

In March, 40 of our members went on an overnight trip to the Baga Retreat Centre, perched on a hill with breathtaking views of Baga Beach and distant dolphins and boats. The centre has beautiful sea-facing rooms. We celebrated Palm Sunday Mass in a stunning chapel, enjoyed insightful talks, simple yet delicious food, and fun games. Some members even ventured down the steep paths for walks. I was delighted to celebrate my 70th birthday at the centre. Everyone enjoyed the stay so much that no one wanted to leave!

Among our members is the incredible Fatima D'Cunha, who is blind but never misses an event. She participates in all the games, sings, and dances wonderfully. Dancing the jive with her was an unforgettable experience. Fatima worked in a hospital and even creates spontaneous Konkani songs. She truly inspires us all.

In April 2024 we completed 10 years with the seniors, and I am looking forward to the Club's 5th Anniversary in August 2024.

The journey of "The Sizzling Seniors Club" has been filled with laughter, companionship, and a deep sense of community. Each event brings us closer together, proving that age is just a number when you're surrounded by friends and fun.

Sizzling Seniors

Featured in
The Goan magazine

Business Minded

Chapter 21

Embracing Life's Challenges

Why would I want to write an autobiography about my life?

To begin with, I was just a simple girl from Bombay, growing up in a middle-class family. My parents weren't highly educated; I don't think they went beyond the fifth standard. But my mother instilled in me the power of prayer. She would always light a lamp and pray. Even today, whenever my kids face problems, they call me and say, "Mum, please light the candle and pray for me." The reason I mention this is because every achievement in my life came with a lot of prayers.

I've been blessed with a very eventful life, and I wanted to document at least an essence of the experiences I've had. If anyone reading this book feels inspired to take life by the horns, my purpose will be fulfilled. My mantra has always been, "If I want, I can still do it!" Each endeavour was challenging, some serving as '*a means to an end*', others fuelling my passion for the arts, and some simply giving back to the society that has been a part of my life in Goa.

Fred Astaire once received the audition remark: "Slightly bald but can dance a little."

Steve Jobs was a college dropout.

So, what was holding me back from being more than I could be?

While I only completed my SSC (Secondary School Certificate), I like to think I've done a "triple graduation" with my three kids. Ha! Ha! So, there was nothing stopping me from achieving whatever I set my mind to.

From a young age, my father taught us the value of money and how to save for a rainy day. We didn't have any godfathers or easy money. Every rupee was earned through "blood, sweat, and tears." My mother also instilled in us the belief that no sincere and heartfelt prayer goes unanswered. Throughout my life, I've witnessed many instances that can only be described as miracles, where blessings arrived just when they were needed.

I Believe in Miracles ...

My Singing Career – A Journey of Passion

My singing career was built on prayers, hours of practice, patience, and dedication. It became my passion. I want to inspire readers that **hard work is essential in whatever you do**.

My mother's words still ring true: "***Whatever you do, do it well or don't do it at all***."

Of course, she was a Perfectionist!

The Video Library – Desperate Times Call for Desperate Measures

In a country like Saudi Arabia, where women had to be covered and couldn't drive, and the government only allowed women to work in banks and schools, I had to **think outside the box**.

Back then, video libraries didn't exist in Saudi Arabia, so it was an ideal business to start.

The Regal Circulating Library – Nothing as Regal as Owning a Library

Even though my time with the library was short, I **met many new people and developed a clientele** for my next business venture.

The Garage Sale – Making the Best of What You Have

When my stint in the library business ended, I wondered what to do with all the leftover books. I had to **get creative**. The answer was simple: Sell Them!

During this process, I met many Gulf expats who had settled in Goa after the Gulf War. They had lots of extra household items, especially crockery and electronics, they didn't know what to do with. Then it struck me—I had the space to sell, and they had the materials. That's how "Seconds to Go" was born.

Seconds to Go - Turning Unwanted Items into Unexpected Treasures

The arrangement was simple: clients would price their items and give me 10% of the selling price for using my space and, of course, my excellent selling skills! Although my shop started with humble beginnings, over the course of 20 years, it grew from selling household items to even handling queries about selling homes and cars. Ha! Ha! I had to develop a keen sense of **interpreting my customers needs**.

The Goa Talent Seekers – Galaxies in Stardust

With my singing background, I thought I could help kids showcase their talents. **Drawing from personal experience**, I decided I could teach them how to sing through a non-profit organization. I envisioned different categories of talent, from primary school to college level. It required hours of hard work, patience, commitment, and dedication.

The Sizzling Seniors Club – Age Isn't Everything!

If I could do something for the children, why not for the Seniors?

Social work brings a lot of happiness, and not everything is about money. Without any business qualifications or financial background, I knew I could bring joy to many seniors. All it took was bringing them together and giving them a good time.

A Life Filled with Blessings

As I reflect on my life, I realize how blessed I've been with wonderful experiences and incredible people.

Writing this autobiography is my way of sharing the essence of my journey. I hope it inspires others to embrace life's challenges with determination and faith.

No matter where you come from or what obstacles you face, with **Prayer, Hard work, and a little bit of Faith … <u>Anything is Possible</u>**.